Records
Management

RECORDS MANAGEMENT

Second Edition

Policies

•

Practices

•

Technologies

SUSAN Z. DIAMOND, COAP

amacom

American Management Association

This book is available at a special
discount when ordered in bulk quantities.
For information, contact Special Sales Department,
AMACOM, a division of American Management Association,
135 West 50th Street, New York, NY 10020.

This publication is designed to provide accurate and
authoritative information in regard to the subject matter
covered. It is sold with the understanding that the publisher is
not engaged in rendering legal, accounting, or other professional
service. If legal advice or other expert assistance is required, the
services of a competent professional person should be sought.

Library of Congress Cataloging-in-Publication Data

Diamond, Susan Z.
    Records management : policies, practices, technologies /
Susan Z. Diamond. —2nd ed.
    p.   cm.
    Includes bibliographical references and index.
    ISBN 0-8144-5028-8
    1. Records—Management.   I. Title.
HF5736.D48   1991   91-53054
651.5—dc20   CIP

Printing number

10 9 8 7 6 5 4

To
Allan

Contents

Preface

As I began revising this book, two facts stood out. First, the basic principles of records management remain unchanged. They remain unchanged for a reason—they work. Second, in the seven years since the first edition was published, the technology and resources available to the records manager have changed dramatically.

While records management has always been a challenging and rewarding profession, now is an especially exciting time for records managers. New technological innovations are being announced daily—innovations full of promise but also full of potential pitfalls. The records manager must integrate tried and proven concepts with these innovations and construct an effective program that meets his or her organization's specific needs.

The ideas in this book have been tested repeatedly through my consulting practice and communicated to thousands of participants in American Management Association seminars. I am grateful to all of the individuals I've worked with for the interchange of ideas, as well as for the continued enthusiasm and support for this book.

Thanks are also due to Gifford R. Salisbury, CRM, who provided valuable insights and feedback in his review of the manuscript, and to Myles Thompson, my editor at AMACOM and the motivating force behind this second edition. I am also grateful to the following companies for providing the photographs for this edition: Commercial Archives, Eastman Kodak Company, Minolta Corporation, Tab Products Company, and 3M.

Finally, this book is dedicated to my husband. For almost twenty years, Allan has encouraged and supported me in every venture I have undertaken. We are a team, and this book is his as well as mine.

Susan Z. Diamond

1

The Role of Records Management

Records management. The words conjure up a variety of meanings: a fancy name for filing; the storage of inactive records; the computerization of information; microfilming; records retention schedules. Actually records management is all of the above and much more. But while records management has been around for a number of years, many organizations either still do not have a viable program or have allowed an existing one to become dormant. Before considering why this situation has occurred and what needs to be done to correct it, we need to establish exactly what records management is.

Let's begin with some key definitions. A *record* is any form of recorded information. The information may be recorded on paper, microfilm, audiotapes, videotapes, or any computer-readable medium such as a computer tape or disk, a compact disk, or an optical disk. In other words, except for unrecorded conversations, practically any information created or communicated within an organization forms a record.

Records typically have a four-stage life cycle. First is *creation*, when pen is put to paper, data are generated by a computer, or information is captured on film, tape, or any other medium. Next is the *period of active use*, which can range from a few days to several years. During this period, users frequently reference the record, so they need quick access to it. Consequently, the record is maintained in the office area. Most records have an active life of one to two years, although there are some obvious exceptions, e.g., a personnel file, which is active as long as the employee is on staff.

The third period in the cycle is *inactivity*, when the record is in storage. During this period, the record is kept either because of legal reasons or because of users' infrequent reference needs. Some records have no inactive period, while others may remain in this stage for several years or even permanently (that is, for the life of the organization).

The final stage in the cycle is *destruction*, which occurs when the organization no longer needs the record and is no longer required by law to keep it. With confidential or proprietary records, special precautions must be taken to ensure that destruction is total and that the records can in no way be re-created.

A common misconception is that records management involves only the latter two stages of a record's life. In reality, records management is a total concept: You are concerned with controlling records from their creation through both active and inactive periods to their destruction. When properly implemented, this total concept means preventing the creation of unnecessary records and unnecessary extra copies, ensuring the efficient, economical use of records in both the active and inactive periods, and destroying records as soon as they're no longer needed. Thus, records management has the dual goals of promoting the efficient retrieval and use of information and keeping records maintenance costs to a minimum, goals that are not mutually exclusive.

Areas of Records Management

With the comprehensive definition I've just outlined, records management becomes a broad-based discipline comprised of the following:

- *Records retention* (keeping records only as long as they are needed)
- *The records center* (the storage area for inactive records)
- *Vital records* (protection of records essential to the organization's continued existence)
- *Filing systems* (the management of active paper records)
- *Document imaging technologies such as micrographics and optical disk* (systems that expedite retrieval of records and conserve space)
- *Forms management* (the proper design and use of forms — one way of controlling records from their creation)
- *Reports management* (the effective design and use of reports—another way to control records from their creation)

Although some records management programs do not encompass all of these areas, ideally all of these functions should be grouped together to enhance overall effectiveness. For example, forms management is most effective when it is part of records management. Not only are the overall goals of both programs quite similar, but poorly designed forms can create major problems in the filing, document imaging, and records storage areas.

Some definitions of records management are even broader, encompassing areas such as mail and messenger service, the print shop, word processing, and copiers. While all of these may be controlled by the records manager under the more general title of administrative services, they are not really part of the records management function. The records manager will, of course, need to interact as closely with these areas as with the information services or data processing group.

Benefits of Records Management to the Organization

Instituting a records management program results in both immediate and long-term benefits to the organization. These benefits include:

• *Faster retrieval of information.* Retrieval speed is improved through both the use of nonpaper-based technology and better management of paper records systems.

• *Fewer lost or misplaced records.* Because the human element is always with us, even the best system in the world will occasionally have a misplaced record. But properly designed document management systems reduce misfiles substantially, and a misfiled record can cost as much as $120 in terms of clerical time spent searching for the record.

• *Compliance with legal retention requirements.* Organizations without a records management program usually do one of two things: Either they run the risk of destroying records too soon and, consequently, can't produce them when legally required, or else they adopt the costly practice of keeping everything forever—a practice that can also backfire in a legal proceeding. If they keep records too long, they must then produce everything they have relating to a proceeding, not just what is legally required. At the very least, producing all related records is time-consuming and expensive and, depending on the nature of the records, may jeopardize the organization's case through the admission of unfavorable evidence.

• *Space savings.* Implementing a records retention schedule and destroying unnecessary and duplicate records can conserve up to 40 percent of the space occupied by records. The effective use of micrographics, high-density filing equipment, and optical disk systems provides further space savings.

• *Reduction of expenditures for filing equipment and supplies.* Eliminating unnecessary records can cut costs dramatically in this area.

• *Control over the creation of new records.* Both forms and reports management reduce the amount of records that are created internally, while improving their effectiveness.

• *Protection of vital records.* No organization is invulnerable to disaster. The destruction of essential records can cost an organization millions of dollars or even prove fatal to its continued existence. A vital records program ensures that the organization has protected copies of these essential records.

The list of benefits provided by a comprehensive records management program is formidable. Together these benefits mean increased efficiency and reduced expense and more than justify the cost and effort required to establish a records management program.

2

Selling the Records Management Concept and Starting the Program

In spite of the benefits records management provides, many records managers find that their biggest problem comes not from implementing the program but from convincing others of the need to implement it. As a records manager, your role as salesperson is further complicated by the fact that two groups must be sold on the concept: (1) upper management and (2) the primary users of the program—middle and lower management and their staffs. Since each group has different concerns, your sales strategy must be modified accordingly.

Selling the Program to Upper Management

If you're having trouble getting senior management to support a records management program, first determine the reasons for their resistance. Usually one or more of the following factors are at the root of the problem:

• *Ignorance of the records management concept.* Most senior managers are only vaguely aware of what records management involves. Consequently, one of your first steps is to educate them in this area.

• *The M word—"money."* Senior managers often don't feel that records management is cost-justified. They think the program will require substantial initial cash outlays with little or no return on the investment. You must show them that while records management is not a profit center, it does save money through greater productivity, more effective use of office space, and reduced expenditures for filing equipment and supplies. Once you emphasize savings, top executives will be much more receptive to the idea.

• *Fear of "empire building."* In highly decentralized organizations, there is often a fear that the records management department will gain too much power or will impede other areas from operating effectively. Here I've found that it helps to compare records management to the human resources and finance areas. I always point out that no company would dream of giving each department head a checkbook and saying, "Pay your own bills." Nor would it let each manager run employment ads in the paper and hire just anyone at any salary level. Likewise, it is not realistic to expect each department head to be an expert in records management. In other words, controls have already been placed over the organization's two most valuable resources, money and people. Records management is a similar control placed over the third key resource, information.

• *Ignorance of the organization's legal vulnerability if it doesn't have a program.* As legal protection, records management is similar to an insurance policy: You hope you never have to use it, but if you do, you're really glad you have it. When companies are involved in litigation, fast and complete retrieval of relevant records is essential. Also, a consistent records management program helps protect the company from charges of destroying or misplacing records to conceal information. In fact, as records manager, you may even be required to testify about the company's record retention policies and procedures. Because of these factors, many organizations belatedly establish records management after litigation occurs. A little forethought in this area would have saved them considerable effort and expense in document production.

• *No awareness that problems exist.* In other words, "We've always managed just fine without a records management program." But remember, senior managers rarely have problems obtaining records. They usually have the best secretarial and administrative support in the organization. When they need a record, they get it. Heaven and earth may have been moved to provide it, but the executives are blissfully unaware of that fact.

Also symptoms of a records management problem such as a shortage of office space, rising copier costs, and increased filing equipment expenditures are rarely linked together. Instead, they are treated separately through such remedies as open-plan offices, new types of filing equipment, and copier controls. While these solutions may be advisable, the first step should be to deal with the underlying problem—the lack of records management.

If management is unaware of the problems, collect your data. Document the difficulties that have occurred, and demonstrate how the records management program will resolve these problems.

Shaping a Strategy

After you've determined why management at your organization either has not established a records management program or has allowed an existing program to become inactive, you can develop an appropriate sales strategy. Keep in mind the needs and concerns of the people you must convince. For example, if management is concerned with being "state of the art," emphasize technological innovations such as optical disk systems. On the other hand, if it is conservative or resistant to change, emphasize the legal problems the company could encounter without a records management program. For both groups, providing reinforcement through examples of what other organizations are doing is important—in the one case, because it shows how other companies are keeping up-to-date, in the other, because it defuses any management suspicions of "empire building" and substantiates your recommendations. You might arrange to visit a company with a comprehensive, well-run records management program. Other options are to provide managers with appropriate articles on the subject or to take them to a local meeting of the Association of Records Managers and Administrators (ARMA) International.

If cost justification is a prime concern, it helps to document expenditures for filing equipment over the past five years and the cost of the office space now occupied by that filing equipment. Then point out that implementing a records management program will make approximately 40 percent of the space available for other uses and may eliminate the need to purchase filing equipment for several years.

Also, any significant capital expenditure should be cost-justified (cost-benefit analyses will be discussed throughout this book in relation to each aspect of the program). Showing senior management that you understand the economic realities is extremely important in getting financial support for the program.

One last psychological point: Don't criticize the company's previous records management practices—or lack thereof; the people you are trying to convince may have sanctioned those practices. Instead, take the approach that the existing system undoubtedly met the organization's needs initially but is no longer adequate in view of such factors as the changing legal climate or the increased cost of office space.

Gathering Data

If you still encounter resistance to establishing a program, a survey of current records management practices within your organization should provide the data to get the support you need. This survey is not a comprehensive study of the organization's records (that comes later when you're preparing the retention schedule) but a means of identifying major records problems within the organization and providing some statistical support for the program.

Unless you're with a very small organization, gathering data through interviews will be too time-consuming. Surveying the departments via a questionnaire (see Exhibit 2-1) is usually more practical. One caution here: Keep the questionnaire short and

Exhibit 2-1.   Sample Departmental Records Management Survey Form.

DEPARTMENTAL RECORDS MANAGEMENT SURVEY	
Dept. Name	Dept. No.
Survey Completed By	Date

1. What volume of paper records are now maintained in your department? Indicate the number on the appropriate line(s).
   _____ file drawers   _____ shelves
   _____ boxes (box size: _____)
   other: _____

2. Has the volume of records increased in the past year?
   ☐ Yes   ☐ No   If yes, by what amount?_____

3. If you know, state approximately how much money your department has spent on filing equipment and supplies in each of the past three years.
   1991: _____ 1990: _____ 1989: _____

4. How many years of records does your department maintain in the office area?
   ☐ 1 to 2   ☐ 3 to 4   ☐ 5 to 7   ☐ 8 or more

5. Who is responsible for filing records in the department?
   Job title(s): _____

6. If you have any written filing procedures, files indexes, etc., please attach a copy.

7. Is the department experiencing any problems with its records?
   ☐ Yes   ☐ No

   If yes, please indicate the type of problem:
   ☐ lost or missing files   ☐ lack of space for records
   ☐ filing backlogs   ☐ other: _____

   Thank you for your input!

simple. One company I know began its program with a forty-page questionnaire! Needless to say, everyone was sick of records management before the program even got started.

The responses to the questionnaire should provide some effective, attention-getting statistics. For example, one records manager I know was able to point out to the board of directors that there were seven file drawers of records for every office employee and that reducing that number to three and a half drawers would free up enough floor space for eleven additional clerical workstations. Since the company was growing rapidly and had little space, she got management's attention very quickly.

The survey will also allow you to identify which departments generate the most records, which ones experience the most growth in records volume, and which ones have problems or are poorly organized. In most organizations, approximately one-half of the records are in the finance and accounting area. Other typical high-volume areas are research, customer records, legal, human resources, and engineering. These high-volume, high-growth areas are usually the best places to begin converting records to another medium such as microfilm or optical disk; they also offer the greatest potential for space savings through disposition of unnecessary and duplicate records.

An area that is poorly organized and is experiencing problems with its record keeping should be a high priority for attention. Of course, the politics of the situation will affect this as well. A department that realizes it has problems and wants help is much easier to work with than one that feels it has no problems. Since you want to build credibility for the program through successes, start with the people who want help.

If, instead of starting from scratch, you've inherited an existing program, you may want to begin by surveying departments to find out what parts of the program are working for them. Obviously, the nature of this survey will depend on the kind of program in place, but Exhibit 2-2 is a typical sample.

Developing an Action Plan

As any records manager with a good program can tell you, establishing a full-scale program usually takes years. However, before

Exhibit 2-2.   Sample Departmental Records Management Survey
Form for a program already in place.

DEPARTMENTAL RECORDS MANAGEMENT SURVEY

Dept. Name	Dept. No.
Survey Completed By	Date

1. Does your department have a copy of the corporate records
    manual?
    ☐ Yes   ☐ No
2. Are the records maintained in the office purged regularly in
    accordance with the retention schedule?
    ☐ Yes   ☐ No   If yes, who does it?
    Job title(s): _____
3. Does your department send inactive reports to the corporate
    records center?
    ☐ Yes   ☐ No   If yes, how often?
    ☐ monthly   ☐ quarterly   ☐ annually   other: _____
4. How frequently does your department retrieve records from the
    corporate records center?
    ☐ weekly   ☐ monthly   ☐ quarterly   ☐ annually   ☐ never
5. If you retrieve records, how long does it normally take to receive a
    record?
    ☐ 4 hrs. or less   ☐ 4 to 8 hrs.   ☐ over 1 day
6. Have you ever not received a record you requested?
    ☐ Yes   ☐ No   If yes, how often in the past year?
    ☐ once   ☐ twice   ☐ 3 or more times
    What reason was given? _____
7. Do you have any comments or suggestions for improving the records
    management program?

    _____
    _____
    _____
    _____
    _____

Thank you for your comments!

you panic or consider the task hopeless, remember that within as little as one year, significant improvements can be made and a firm foundation laid for the overall program.

Your first step is to identify what needs to be done and establish priorities. If your company has no records retention schedule or if an existing schedule has not been revised within the past two years, your first stop is to prepare or update the schedule. If a current schedule exists, you'll need to decide what area is most critical; your survey data should help you make this decision.

Every records manager I've ever known has had to struggle with limited staff and monetary resources. Therefore, develop your program in stages; if you try to advance in too many areas at once, you'll be unsuccessful in all of them. Also, grandiose plans tend to make senior management nervous. A better way is to first outline to management the overall strategy for the entire program in general terms, then identify immediate priorities and the benefits the program will provide, and finally explain how you will accomplish your priority goals. By asking for approval on a step-by-step basis, you stand a much greater chance of getting it.

If management is still hesitant, I've found it helps to use the words *pilot program*. Somehow, a pilot program doesn't sound so irrevocable, and it indicates you will be receptive to reevaluation and modification of the program as needed. I've also found it helpful to supplement a written action plan with visual aids. Photographs of the collapsing cartons in the company's records center are the best argument you can make for purchasing shelving for that area. Photographs of records stored in cardboard boxes in closets and stacked on top of overflowing cabinets in the office area also provide vivid testimony that a problem exists. But be sure you have permission from the heads of the departments you photograph so they won't think you're trying to embarrass them.

In addition to photographs of problem areas, also include in your action plan illustrations of any new equipment to be purchased. Floor plans showing how much space will be opened up provide further support. It also helps to present senior management with a time line or milestone chart (see Exhibit 2-3) indicating how long it will take to accomplish each step of the project and which employees' cooperation will be needed. Such a chart

Exhibit 2-3. Sample Milestone Chart, filled in.

PROJECT PLAN	Project Title RECORDS RETENTION SCHEDULE	Objectives Develop a records retention schedule for XYZ Co.		Date 8/20/91 Page 1 of 1

Task	Description	Performed By	Month 1	Month 2	Month 3	Month 4	Month 5	Month 6
1	Send memo to department heads.	CEO/ Rec. Mgr.	◁					
2	Select records coordinators.	Dept. Heads	◁					
3	Prepare records inventory form.	Rec. Mgr.	●					
4	Set up retention database.	Rec. Mgr./ MIS	●					
5	Train records coordinators.	Rec. Mgr.	●					
6	Conduct inventory of departments.	Rec. Coords.	◁					
7	Review inventory data.	Rec. Mgr.		◁				
8	Input data into database.	Rec. Asst.		●				
9	Prepare draft retention schedule / procedure.	Rec. Mgr.		●				
10	Review schedule (department heads).	Dept. Heads			●			
11	Amend schedule as needed.	Rec. Mgr.			◁			
12	Review & approve schedule (corporate legal).	Gen. Counsel				●		
13	Amend schedule as needed.	Rec. Mgr.				●		
14	Review & approve schedule (sr. mgmt.).	CEO/VPs					●	
15	Amend schedule as needed.	Rec. Mgr.					◁	
16	Publish schedule & procedures.	Rec. Mgr./ Print Shop						●

Note: This example covers only the preparation of a retention schedule, not the implementation. Actual time required to perform various tasks varies from organization to organization.

also helps to correct unrealistic assumptions as to how long it will take to implement the program or what resources will be needed. And if you can get potential users of the program to comment on the current records problems they face and how the program will benefit them, your case will be greatly strengthened.

If you don't gain immediate approval, don't give up. Instead, analyze the objections and develop appropriate responses or modify your proposal accordingly. For example, if the objection is cost, analyze the proposal to see where costs could be trimmed and what the ultimate effect would be. Perhaps less equipment could be installed initially or the equipment could be leased.

Getting Cooperation From Users

Although upper management support is essential for implementing the program, you'll also need backing and cooperation from the program's users. Users can and do sabotage management-approved programs when they perceive those programs as being unworthy of their support. Just as you did with senior management, you'll need to determine the causes for any user resistance to records management. Usually the most basic cause is fear— fear of losing control of their records or fear that a critical record will not be found when it's needed. I call this the Linus syndrome. In the comic strip *Peanuts*, Linus clings to his security blanket; most users feel the same way about their records.

Alleviating these fears is a matter of education and user involvement. As an initial step, have each department appoint a records coordinator to serve as a liaison between the records management group and the other members of his or her department. The coordinator should be someone who works well with others and has a good rapport with the rest of the department. He or she should also be receptive to new ideas, be able to coordinate details well, and have been with the department for at least one year. It also helps if this person is at least at the administrative assistant level or higher.

Although all managers need general information about the records management program, you'll work most closely with department heads and records coordinators. Department heads are responsible for making sure that you get full cooperation from their departments. To help ensure such support, it's a good idea to draft a memo (see Exhibit 2-4) for the signature of the president (or another top executive) that states why the records management program is being implemented and asks everyone involved to give you their full support. If you draft the memo, it's much more likely to be sent than if you just ask the executive to write it.

Your credibility with users will increase gradually. If you can substantially help one department, word will spread, and other departments will be more receptive to the program. It's also helpful to get the records management program featured in the company newspaper or magazine. Editors of such publications are usually looking for material; "before and after" photographs are especially effective here. And, of course, a good program is its own best sales tool. Once people realize the benefits, they'll support the program.

An Ongoing Sales Effort

Promoting your records management program is not a onetime task. If the program is to be a success, effort must be applied steadily and consistently. The problem many organizations encounter is that after the initial push to get such a program up and running, records management begins to lose priority. Funds and resources are cut; the program loses momentum and effectiveness. After several years of slipping, someone again recognizes that the organization has a "records problem," another major effort is begun, and the cycle starts over again.

If you have inherited a moribund program, first find out what caused the program to fade away. Then as you begin to resuscitate it, be sure to stress why your version is different and the steps you have taken to ensure the program's continued life.

It's your responsibility to ensure that the program remains a priority item and does not slip into oblivion. To achieve this goal, keep management aware of your accomplishments on an ongoing basis. Also look for ways to expand the program and improve its effectiveness.

Exhibit 2-4. Example of a memo from senior management discussing why program is being implemented.

TO: All Department Heads   DATE: March 13, 19x2

FROM: Catharine de Bourgh, CEO

SUBJECT: Establishment of a Records Management Program

During the upcoming months, we will be establishing a records management program at XYZ Co. This program will:

- Ensure that we comply with all legal and regulatory record retention requirements
- Enable us to identify and protect those records that are essential to the corporation
- Improve the retrieval of records
- Allow us to develop strategies to manage the rapid growth of our records
- Conserve valuable office space through the off-site storage of inactive records and the destruction of duplicate and unnecessary records

Elizabeth Bennet, manager, office services, is responsible for establishing and maintaining the records management program. To ensure that the program meets your department's needs, I am asking you to appoint a records coordinator for your area.

While serving as coordinator will not require a major time commitment, it is a critical position. The coordinator will be your department's liaison in this area and will thus ensure that the program addresses the concerns of you and your staff. Therefore, the coordinator should have a good overall knowledge of your department's operation. Possibly, the department's administrative assistant would be a good candidate.

Initially we will ask the coordinators to gather some brief but essential information on the categories of records maintained in your area and your department's requirements for those records. Elizabeth will meet with the coordinators to explain exactly what information is needed and will provide guidance as needed during the process. These data will be used to prepare a records retention schedule for the company.

(continues)

Exhibit 2-4.   (*continued*).

Please let Elizabeth know your choice for coordinator by {*date*}. Also, if
you have any questions about the program, please contact Elizabeth. I
appreciate you cooperation in this critical activity.

One thing that keeps awareness up is having training sessions for new employees. Another is holding periodic open
houses. For example, if you've opened a new central file area or
installed a new imaging system, invite people to view the facility
to see how it works. One of my clients served champagne at the
open house—I assure you that that does wonders for attendance.
But even serving coffee and cookies is an incentive.

Ongoing user cooperation is also essential. Users must be
aware that you will be responsive to their needs and interested in
improving the program whenever possible. When new department heads and records coordinators are appointed, your group
should train them in the program instead of letting them assimi-
late it gradually, and often incorrectly, on their own.

Such ongoing efforts make the company's initial investment
in people, time, and money worthwhile and ensure the continued effectiveness of the program.

3

Developing and Staffing the Records Management Program

Records management used to be one of those functions few people wanted responsibility for. As a result, one of three things tended to happen: The organization abdicated responsibility altogether by stating that each department was responsible for developing and maintaining its own records management program, assigned the responsibility to whoever did want it, or placed it in the administrative services area (not necessarily a bad decision).

Today, organizations are more aware of the importance of their records; also document imaging technology such as optical disk systems has added some "sex appeal" to records management. As a result, more thought is being given to the decision on where to position records management.

Since it is critical that the records management function be centralized within the corporation, expecting each department to develop expertise in this area is unrealistic. However, a large corporation may need to delegate responsibility to individual divisions or subsidiaries, specifying that they develop their own program within corporate guidelines and subject to corporate approval.

The Buck Stops Where?

But which department should have overall accountability? The decision is no longer a simple one. As mentioned, the traditional place for records management is in the administrative services area along with such functions as reprographics, the mail room, facilities management, and office supplies. There is a certain logic to this approach, as records management is also a support function that crosses departmental lines and provides service throughout the organization. Grouping these areas together increases the likelihood that users will receive efficient, comprehensive administrative services from a department that is accustomed to assisting others and that perceives such assistance as its primary function.

However, because records management has become increasingly automated, it is now not uncommon to find it as part of Information Services Systems (IS) or Management Information Systems (MIS)—i.e., data processing or the "computer" department. This grouping has the obvious advantage of giving the records management function direct access to strong technical support. The possible disadvantage is that paper is still a heavy component of any records management program and data processing personnel may be uncomfortable or unfamiliar with paper-based systems.

Whether or not records management is part of IS/MIS, the two areas must work closely together to ensure smooth implementation of computerized records management systems and the inclusion of electronic records in the overall records management program.

While records management is most commonly part of administrative services or IS/MIS, it may also be found under the auspices of the legal or finance departments, the corporate secretary's office, or the library. I used to question the rationale behind these groupings. However, having seen records managers function successfully as a part of all of these areas, I've come to the conclusion that it's not where on the organization chart the function is but its backing by top management that makes the difference.

Staffing the Program—Managers

Once the basic idea of a central or corporate records management program has been accepted, staffing on both the managerial and clerical levels becomes a key issue.

First question whether you really need a full-time records manager. Many smaller organizations (typically 500 employees or fewer) do function successfully with a records manager who has other duties. However, the program itself is usually relatively simple, and the records manager has a clerical support staff that devotes part of its time to the program. Larger organizations and any organization making an aggressive effort to reduce paper and increase control over records usually need a full-time records manager.

The next question is, Where do you find a records manager? While the number of records managers is increasing steadily, so is the number of companies needing them. However, if your company is willing to provide sufficient compensation, a qualified records manager can usually be hired away from another firm.* When bringing in someone from outside, the company may not only resist the records management concept but distrust the newcomer. Consequently, in addition to professional competence in records management, the person brought in needs strong leadership qualities and an ability to sell the program.

One way to locate such an individual is to advertise either in the ARMA International newsletter, *News: Notes and Quotes,* or in newsletters of local ARMA chapters. Since ARMA is the professional organization of records managers, you can contact virtually all available qualified individuals at a relatively minimal cost. (ARMA International's address, as well as those of other related professional organizations, is found in the Resources section at the end of this book.)

Your other alternative is to train someone from within the organization to handle the job. This is a workable solution, since

---

*While compensation varies with region and responsibilities, according to the Administrative Management Society's *1990 AMS Management Salaries Report,* $32,300 was the average salary for a records manager in the United States.

unlike accountants and engineers, many highly qualified records managers acquire most of their expertise on the job.

Of course, the new records manager will need a concentrated training program through seminars and reading books such as this one. Or he or she may want to take one of the many courses in records management being offered at colleges and universities. If taught by a practicing records manager or someone with extensive practical experience, such courses can be valuable. But check the instructor's background; such courses are sometimes taught by individuals who have no hands-on experience.

Some companies hire consultants to establish the program and get it up and running. If you choose this approach, be sure your staff has input in developing the program and acquires the expertise necessary to manage the program after the consultant's work is done.

Staffing the Program—Clerical Personnel

Of course, records management programs require more than just managers. You may need filing personnel, micrographics/document imaging equipment operators, data entry individuals, and other records center staff. Since most of these positions primarily require on-the-job training, finding qualified personnel is relatively easy. Keeping them is another matter.

Several factors are responsible for the high turnover. One is low salaries; other types of work requiring comparable experience often pay better. Another is that as individuals' skills improve, they often move on to better-paying positions. A third reason is that the work is often monotonous and boring. And finally, these positions are perceived as lacking in prestige, and people working in them receive little, if any, respect from others in the company. Remarks such as "Have the *girls* check the files" or "Have the *boy* get the box from the records center" are indicative of this problem.

Although new technology has changed the nature of the positions, the need to fill these jobs doesn't go away. Instead of more filing personnel, you may need more people doing data entry. Instead of more camera operators, you may need people to run document scanners. The jobs are changing, but they are still highly repetitive.

And although these jobs are routine, they are also essential and must be performed well. If there is continual turnover, you'll be constantly training new personnel—an expensive, time-consuming process—and monitoring quality control more closely.

But the situation is not hopeless. By adopting a combination of the strategies outlined below, you can resolve these problems. Here are two things you can do:

1. *Upgrade both job titles and salaries.* According to the Administrative Management Society's *1990 AMS Office, Professional, and Data Processing Salaries Report*, a file clerk in the United States receives an average salary of $13,400, while a data entry operator receives $15,800. Such salaries are, of course, strong incentives to look for other jobs. At the very least, your records personnel should receive pay comparable to that offered by other companies in the area for similar positions, and ideally the salaries should be greater.

When upgrading job titles, try to eliminate the words *files* and *clerk*. Both have negative connotations. Since we no longer deal only with paper, substitute *records* or *documentation* for *files*. Alternatives for *clerk* are *specialist, analyst, coordinator,* or *technician*, depending on the exact nature of the position. Admittedly, you can't deposit a job title in the bank. But upgrading titles makes it easier to improve compensation and helps increase self-esteem.

2. *Create career paths.* The best way to keep qualified individuals within the records management area is to provide advancement opportunities. For example, a new staff member might begin as a records analyst trainee and be promoted in three months to a records analyst if the filing systems are mastered. Then, nine months later, he or she could become a senior records analyst and acquire additional responsibilities. But for this system to work, the titles should be linked to specific increases in responsibility as well as salary, and the career path should permit qualified individuals to move into supervisory positions when an appropriate opening occurs.

But upgrading positions and salaries does not solve the whole problem of high turnover. You will also need to make the jobs more interesting. A few people can file, film, or do data entry quite happily all day and not mind the monotony, but most workers become bored, and the quality of their work suffers. Here are three motivational approaches for reducing the monotony:

1. *Job enrichment*—having one person perform several actions that comprise a complete process rather than the same action over and over. As a result, the individual assumes more control over and responsibility for his or her work. For example, in a plant, a team of workers might build a major portion of the product, which does not occur when the assembly-line method is used.

Job enrichment can be applied on a smaller scale as well. For example, instead of having everyone file throughout the file area, assign portions of the files to various employees and have each one assume responsibility for the maintenance of his or her files. This approach tends to increase the employees' interest in their work because they learn an area thoroughly. Filing is done more carefully because employees know that they personally will have to cope with any problems caused by their misfiles. And when errors do occur, you can easily trace them to their source and work with that employee to correct the problem.

2. *Cross-training*—teaching employees to perform more than one job. For example, files personnel can learn how to prepare documents for scanning or microfilming. This breaks the monotony of filing. Cross-training personnel also means that you have trained "backups" available if someone is on vacation or ill. One caution: Some union situations make it difficult or even impossible to cross-train employees.

3. *Forming a quality circle within your department.* Admittedly, this is primarily a tool for larger records management departments, since at least four or five employees in addition to a manager or supervisor are needed for an effective quality circle.

The group should meet regularly—perhaps every two weeks or once a month—to discuss ways to improve the department's efficiency or resolve problems. Keep in mind that the meeting is not a "bitch" session where everyone ventilates frustrations but one directed toward solutions. Its purpose is to look at both large and small issues. Members should feel comfortable bringing up simple concepts—labeling file shelves differently—as well as complex issues—dealing with records center users who don't follow departmental procedures. Since some people may initially feel reluctant to express themselves, ask everyone to write down two or three ideas for improving departmental operations or to list some topics for discussion and turn them in to the group leader. These can provide a good starting point for the discussion.

Quality circles also promote team building within the department. Individuals from one area, such as filing, become familiar with the problems and issues faced by other areas, such as microfilming or data entry, as well as learning how what they do affects others.

Activities such as cross-training and quality circles help you identify qualified staff members who can move into supervisory positions. Promoting from within shows that career paths really do exist.

Alternative Sources of Personnel

Having read this far, you may be thinking, "My problem isn't turnover; I don't have any staff to turn over. How do I get approval to add staff?" At many companies, the standard response to the request for staff is "We don't want to add head count." And the records manager understandably feels frustrated when he or she has prepared five pages of carefully worded justification explaining exactly what the new person will do and why the position is essential, only to be told, "No new FTEs [full-time employees]."

Now it's time to drop back and punt. If you can't get full-time staff, consider part-time personnel. Part-time staff is often easier to justify, since the company does not have to pay benefits and can terminate them easily if costs have to be cut. One viable alternative is to hire retired employees to work a limited number of hours. Many retired individuals want to supplement their income and make very conscientious, highly motivated staff members. Another is to consider individuals whose children may be in school and would like to work part-time. High school work-study programs are another possibility. Finally, if a local college or university offers courses in records management, consider sponsoring an internship. An intern works part-time and writes a paper based on the experience gained on the job.

Temporary agencies are another source of personnel. Quite frankly, I'm ambivalent on this one. Some of my clients have found outstanding staff members this way. On the other hand, by the time you get the temporary trained, he or she may have moved on to another job or left the agency. You also have to be sure the person has adequate skills. Unfortunately, literacy is not something you can take for granted, so check any new individual's work carefully.

One other source of personnel—both full- and part-time— deserves mention. Consider hiring physically or mentally disabled individuals for certain positions. Individuals who are hearing-impaired or unable to walk can operate a microfilm camera or perform data entry with no difficulty. Preparing documents for microfilming and certain types of routine filing are tasks that some mentally handicapped persons can handle very well.

Since there are affirmative action programs for hiring handicapped staff, your personnel department should be able to assist you in finding qualified candidates. Shelter workshops and social agencies are also good sources of referrals. Some of these groups even operate microfilming service bureaus and can provide trained micrographics personnel.

Of course, qualified individuals with disabilities should move upward along the records management career path in the same way other department members do.

Remember, whatever the job title or pay scale, your employees should be treated with respect and courtesy, both by you and by others in the company. It's your responsibility to establish a precedent here by referring to employees by their names or job titles, not as "the girls" or "the boys," and by making sure that others within the company treat them with similar courtesy.

Professional Staff Development

Records management is a rapidly changing field—particularly in the technological area. As a result, both records managers and their staffs need to devote considerable time and effort to professional growth and development. Membership in ARMA International is an excellent first step. For a modest annual fee, members receive the *Records Management Quarterly*, as well as newsletters and chapter publications. Membership also includes the opportunity to join an industry action committee (IAC) comprised of records managers in specific industries such as pharmaceuticals, utilities, state government, and banking/financial services. Of course, the most valuable aspect of membership is the opportunity to meet and exchange ideas with others in the same profession through local chapter meetings and regional and national events.

The Resources section at the end of this book also lists a number of other professional organizations of value to the records manager, such as the Association for Information and Image Management (AIIM), the Nuclear Information and Records Management Association (NIRMA), and Office Automation Society International (OASI).

Like many other professions, records management has a certification program, in this case sponsored by the Institute of Certified Records Managers. To become a certified records manager (CRM), you must have a degree from a four-year accredited college and a minimum of three years of full-time professional experience in records management. Or if you have three years of college, you will need five years of records management experience. With a two-year associate degree, seven years of experience is required, and if you have no college, eleven years of experience will be needed. You must also pass a series of examinations on the various aspects of records management.

Another certification possibility is to become a certified office automation professional (COAP), a designation sponsored by OASI. COAP certification is based on the individual's experience in a broad range of office automation areas, including records management.

Whether or not you opt for certification, it is important to keep developing your professional expertise. Attending association meetings and workshops, networking with others in the field, and reading professional journals ensure that you and your program remain state-of-the-art.

4

Records Retention
Conducting the Records Inventory

Now that we've considered where records management belongs in the organization and the proper staffing of the department, you're probably asking, "Where do I start?" You can't institute the entire program at once. And, of course, the exact order of the steps you choose depends on the current status of records management within the organization.

However, if you don't have a records retention schedule or if the one you have has not been revised within the past two years, implementing one is a logical first step, as it enables you to destroy all unnecessary records. Once you've cleared out the deadwood, it's much easier to organize what's left and select appropriate storage and retrieval procedures. In fact, for that reason, records retention is sometimes referred to as records disposition.

Another reason for beginning here is that retention includes inventorying all of the organization's records. And until you know what you have, it's impossible to formulate the rest of the program. Finally, making the retention schedule a high priority demonstrates compliance with the legal retention requirements established by federal, state, and local governments. By implementing a consistent legal program for disposing of records, the company shows that it is not destroying records selectively to conceal evidence. This can be a critical issue if your company becomes involved in litigation.

Successfully implementing records retention is a five-step process:

1. Inventorying the records
2. Determining how long to keep them
3. Preparing the schedule
4. Obtaining approval for the schedule
5. Implementing the schedule

The remainder of this chapter is concerned with the first step—inventorying the records.

The Rationale Behind the Inventory

The records inventory determines what records your company has, where they are located, and how many of them there are. You *cannot* conduct a successful inventory by sending out questionnaires to department heads. Even if they do complete the questionnaires, they are likely to omit some record categories or not supply the necessary level of detail. I'll always remember a form submitted by one department head that listed the record title as "binders" and requested a five-year retention with no indication of what, if anything, was in the binders.

To get meaningful information, a physical inventory must be conducted by properly trained individuals. But before you panic utterly, murmuring "that could take years," let's consider what your goal is. It's not to identify every piece of paper stored in the company or even every different type of document. Instead, it's to identify records *categories* or what's known in records management jargon as *records series*.

For example, the paid invoices in accounts payable are one category. The invoice file might include not only the invoice but also the purchase requisition, purchase order, receiving report, and check copy. However, because these records are filed together and treated as a unit, they make up one category and require only one inventory form. Another example of a category is the employee personnel file. Again, this file contains a number of different documents—e.g., application, résumé, performance appraisals, notices of promotions—but the file itself is a single category. Other record categories, of course, might contain only one type of document, such as canceled checks or employment applications for nonhires.

And remember, you are not inventorying just paper in file folders but also computer printouts, microfilm, magnetic media, photographs, slides, engineering drawings—in short, any recorded information.

Although I've stressed the idea of a comprehensive records inventory, there is one exception: If your company has a number of branch locations or field offices performing the same basic functions and keeping similar records, you need only inventory the records at one or two representative locations.

Collecting the Data

Since one of your goals as records manager is to reduce paper, you may want to consider doing a "paperless" inventory. By this I mean inputting the data directly into the computer instead of using a form—a definite possibility if you have access to a laptop. The sooner you can enter data into a computer, the sooner you can massage and manipulate it. Another paperless alternative is to dictate the data into a portable recorder and have it transcribed directly into the computer (Chapter 5 discusses fields for the retention database and its use).

However, whether you input directly into the computer or use a form as a data collection device, you will need to collect certain information about each record category on a records inventory form (see Exhibit 4-1). If you wish, you may reproduce this form (and all others in this book) for your own use. Or you may prefer to modify it to fit your company's special needs.

Exhibit 4-1. Sample Records Inventory Form.

RECORDS INVENTORY	
Dept. Name	Dept. No.

Record Title

☐ original or "official" copy of record ☐ duplicate

For forms and computer printouts, form or report no.: _____

Description of record and any other comments: _____

_____

_____

_____

Filing equipment type: _____ Filing method:

☐ alphabetic ☐ numeric ☐ date ☐ other: _____

Year	Volume	Activity Level

Media: ☐ paper ☐ microfilm/microfiche ☐ other: _____

Admin. retention (indicate the number of years on the appropriate

lines): _____ in office _____ in storage

Others with copies of record (if known): _____

Inventoried by: _____ Date: _____

= =

To be completed by records management department:

Legal retention: _____

Comments: _____

_____

_____

_____

_____

Final retention decision: _____ in office _____ in storage

Approved by: _____ Date: _____

A review of the inventory items in Exhibit 4-1 indicates the type of information you should collect. For example:

• It's a good idea to obtain both the department name and number (usually the accounting code assigned to that department). It is simpler to organize the schedule by department number, but the name will remind you of the department's actual function.

• In some cases, the title of the record will be obvious—e.g., purchase orders. In others, the title may need clarification. For example, five departments may have "project files," each containing different types of information and referring to different types of projects. More appropriate titles might be "plant maintenance project files" or "telecommunications project files."

Avoid informal names for record titles or organizational slang. I once received an inventory form with the record title "adds and kills." No, the firm wasn't into gang warfare; this was its name for the membership addition and deletion report. Since corporate counsel might have to present the schedule in court, it's good practice to use clear, descriptive titles that don't cause confusion.

If more than one department keeps copies of the record, be sure the same title is used consistently. For example, different departments might refer to the same report as monthly budget reports, summary budget reports, and budget summaries. An appropriate standard title would be "budget reports—departmental—monthly." A separate inventory form should be prepared for each department that has a copy of the record.

• After you've established the title, the next step is to determine whether you are inventorying the *copy of record* or a duplicate copy. The copy of record is the organization's official copy. When this copy is no longer needed in the office, it is placed in inactive storage at the company's records center for the remainder of its life span. Duplicates, however, are only kept in the office for as long as they are needed and then destroyed.

The next question, of course, is how to determine which copy is the copy of record. There is no one answer that always works, but the following guidelines will resolve the issue:

1. If the original is kept within the company, it normally becomes the copy of record.
2. If the original is not kept within the company (e.g., a letter), the originator's copy becomes the copy of record.

If neither of the above conditions is met, then the copy of record is the copy belonging to the department with the greatest need and use for the record or the complete set. For example, the legal department would have the copy of record for "litigation files," and the accounts payable department would have the copy of record for "paid invoices."

Distinguishing between the copy of record and duplicates is essential to ensure that one and only one copy is kept for an extended period. Not only do duplicates waste valuable space, they can cause legal problems. Often, in litigation, the other side will request that all copies of a record in existence be produced. This is done in hopes of finding an incriminating note on one of the copies. Even if your personnel have properly refrained from writing such notes, the mere cost of finding and producing all copies can add substantially to litigation expense. It's much simpler and cheaper if you can show that the retention schedule called for the destruction of duplicates after six months or one year and that the policy was followed.

• The next items on the form provide added clarification. The *form* or *report number,* when one exists, ensures that we're all referring to the same record. The *description* might include a listing of the different types of documents in the file, a brief explanation of how the record is used, and any other pertinent comments. The information on *filing equipment type and method* is primarily of value later in helping departments improve filing practices.

• The next section is critical. For each *year,* you want to find out how much of the record exists and how frequently it is used. Breaking these items down by year lets you determine if the record category is high-volume and growing rapidly and therefore should be converted to another medium. Also if the older years are referenced infrequently, they should be sent to off-site storage unless they occupy very little space.

Volume is measured in several ways. The simplest is to indicate the number of file drawers (e.g., three and a half 36-inch drawers). Another alternative is to measure filing inches or feet; three and a half 36-inch drawers would be 10.5 feet.

The activity level might be daily, weekly, monthly, quarterly, rarely, or never. Breaking it down by year helps clarify at what point the use of the records drops off significantly (usually after the first or second year).

• The media are important because a record may exist in more than one form (e.g., both paper and microfilm). You'll want to indicate on the schedule for how long each form should be kept.

• The administrative retention is how many years the department head wants to keep the record in the office and, if it should go to storage, how many years there. You'll use this information in setting the retention value (see Chapter 5).

• Listing other departments known to have copies of the record makes it easier to determine which copy should be the copy of record; it also ensures that the retention needs of all departments are considered.

The remaining portion of the form is completed by the records management department as part of the process for determining how long the record should be kept.

Who Should Perform the Inventory?

As you've probably guessed by now, inventorying is the most labor-intensive step in preparing the retention schedule. It's also a step you want to complete as quickly as possible. The inventory is equivalent to a photograph of the records, and the more time that elapses, the more things change.

Several alternatives exist for performing the inventory. One, obviously, is for you and your staff to do it, a viable alternative if there is enough staff support and the organization is not too large. This option does ensure high-quality data, and the records management team learns a great deal about the records.

However, many records managers have minimal support staff—and other duties besides records management. If so, sharing the responsibility may be the best alternative. Having each department's records coordinator inventory his or her area expedites the process and ensures that no one person has a large amount to inventory.

If you elect this alternative, you must train the coordinators carefully. They'll need to understand each item on the form. It helps to begin with a group training session where you go over the reasons for preparing the schedule and the inventory form. Follow that by holding a one-on-one session with each individual coordinator in his or her work area. The one-on-one sessions are especially helpful because individuals can show you specific record categories about which they have questions. The downside to this method is that some coordinators may not complete the forms carefully; you'll have to do a certain amount of follow-up to collect all of the data and to resolve inconsistencies or unclear information. However, this method takes less time than doing it yourself, and it does get departments involved in the process.

Another alternative is to have a consultant do the inventorying. Since the consultant has done this many times before, he or she can usually collect the data more quickly than you would. While departments have to spend some time with the consultant, this method requires less effort on their part. Of course, using a consultant increases costs.

Tips on Inventorying

Whichever approach you elect, departments should receive advance notification of the inventory and the reasons for it. Schedule inventories at times that are convenient for the various departments (but don't accept the excuse that no time is convenient). Be sure that the department heads and the secretaries or others responsible for file maintenance will be in the office during the inventory. Then if there is a question about a particular record category, a qualified individual will be present to answer it. Even if the inventory is not being made by a department member, it should be made in the presence of such a person. This practice prevents misunderstanding and ensures that the person doing the inventory is not accused of misplacing or removing records.

Persistence is often necessary to ensure that *all* of the department's records are located. Records don't reside just in file cabinets; they may be found in closets, cartons, storage cabinets, bookcases, and of course people's desks. Obviously, you can't go through someone's desk without permission. But you can ask him or her to show you whatever records are maintained in the desk—feel free to ignore the back issues of *Playboy* or *Cosmopolitan* and other items of a personal nature. Beware, however, of employees who tell you all their records are personal. Work done for the company on company time is not personal.

Subject or Administrative Files

In virtually every department, you'll find a so-called subject, administrative, miscellaneous, or A-to-Z file. This file is an alphabetic collection of "administrivia"—mainly duplicate information or items no one knew where to file but didn't want to destroy. Assigning each such file a separate retention is a lost cause, especially since new files may be created daily.

What I usually do is ask appropriate department personnel if there are any files they wish to keep over two years. If so, these should be assigned a proper retention period and listed separately on the retention schedule. The remaining files can be listed on the schedule as "departmental subject files." The retention should not exceed two years, and the files should not go to storage. One way to ensure that these files don't grow out of proportion is to limit the amount of filing space available for them.

Inventorying Computer-Readable Media

Inventorying paper or microfilm files is relatively simple because you can view the record and determine its contents. However, records kept on a computer present a special challenge.

Let's begin with the computer files maintained by the corporate systems department. If there is already a tape retention schedule listing all the tapes in existence and the retention for each, your task is simply to verify the appropriateness of the retentions. However, most of the time the issue has not been addressed, and the backup tapes are kept indefinitely or "forever."

There are two basic issues with tape retention: disaster recovery—how much backup material do the systems people need to re-create the system in case of a disaster (clearly they have to be the judges of this issue)?—and the users' need for old data. If users simply need to view old reports occasionally, the most cost-effective solution is to generate them on microfiche. However, if they wish to go back and manipulate old data, the information needs to be available on computer-readable media and the retention should be set accordingly.

Unlike paper files, tapes cannot simply be tossed in a box, stored for many years, and then pulled out and reused. Tapes need to be stored in a climate-controlled facility. If a retention of several years is needed, they may need to be rewound or copied at certain intervals to ensure that they remain readable. These are all issues that should be discussed with the systems staff.

And, of course, a tape is useless unless there is equipment to run it on. I find many firms storing old tapes from earlier computer systems—tapes which they no longer have the equipment for. Reviewing tape retentions and adjusting them can save significant amounts of storage costs.

Inventorying the systems group's computer files can be accomplished by working directly with IS/MIS. However, you have only viewed the tip of the iceberg. Most organizations have a large complement of personal computers, loaded with various files. Obviously, there is no way you can keep an up-to-date inventory of all files on PCs.

On the other hand, organizations that totally ignore this records management issue have lived to regret their ostrich approach. Some very critical records may reside on those PCs, and if an individual leaves suddenly, those files may be lost forever. Also, many users either do not back up their PC files regularly or else store the backup next to the PC, so the same disaster, e.g., a fire, could destroy both.

Exhibit 4-2.   Sample Records Inventory Form for individual user
and small-system computer-readable media.

RECORDS INVENTORY FORM FOR INDIVIDUAL USER AND SMALL SYSTEM COMPUTER READABLE MEDIA

Please complete a form for each personal computer file that is of
long-term importance to your department and/or that is updated
regularly or used for an extended period. You do not need to
inventory any files that are on a mainframe or data center system.

Dept. Name	Dept. No.
Your Name	Date

File Title on Computer System

Brief description of file contents and purpose _____

_____

_____

_____

_____

How often is file updated?
☐ daily   ☐ weekly   ☐ monthly   ☐ never
☐ other: _____

How often is file backed up?
☐ daily   ☐ weekly   ☐ monthly   ☐ never
☐ other: _____

Is a backup copy maintained off-site?   ☐ Yes   ☐ No

If yes, where is off-site copy located? _____

Is a hard copy of the file kept also?   ☐ Yes   ☐ No

If yes, where is/are the hard copy/copies kept?
☐ in our department   ☐ other: _____

Hence, it is important to identify critical files kept on PCs and ensure that they are properly backed up. Exhibit 4-2 is a sample inventory form for PC files. This form usually has to be completed by the user, since no one else would have any idea as to the nature of the files on the system or how they are titled.

Since inventorying computer-readable media is a major project in and of itself, you may want to divide the records retention process into two phases. Phase I would be preparing the retention schedule for paper and microfilm records, while Phase II would address magnetic media. Or you may choose to tackle the entire project at once.

Whichever approach you elect, do not ignore computer-readable files. These are just as much company records as paper files. While space savings is not as much of an issue with them, they may be subpoenaed and, in some cases, there are legal requirements as to their retention. And, of course, they are a valuable asset, representing many hours of individuals' time.

What Next?

The inventory is the most labor-intensive part of the retention process. So when you've done this, you've fought half the battle. The next steps, addressed in Chapter 5, are determining how long to keep the records and preparing and implementing the schedule.

5

Records Retention
Preparing and Implementing the Schedule

After the inventory is complete, the records must be appraised, not for their monetary worth but for their value to the organization and, in particular, for the length of time they should be kept.

Values of Records to the Organization

As part of the appraisal process, four types of value must be considered for each record: (1) administrative or operational value; (2) legal value; (3) fiscal/tax value; and (4) historical or archival value.

Let's examine each separately to see how it is determined and who determines it.

Administrative Value

The administrative value of a record is the length of time it may be needed or used within the company. This value is usually set by the department head who is responsible for the copy of record, although the needs of other departments using the record should also be considered.

In addition to an overall retention value, the department head should also set a period of active use. For this period, the record will be kept in the office; then, it will go to the records center for the remainder of the retention period. For most records, the active period should not exceed two years, and it may be substantially less. Of course, there are exceptions, such as an employee's personnel file, which remains active as long as the employee is with the company.

If a manager is unsure about what administrative period to request, approach the issue by asking, "How many years back have you ever referred to this record? Three years? Six years? How important was the referral?"

A few managers feel all of their records should be permanent. *Permanent* is a designation that should be used on a very limited basis. I would push strongly for a specific time period, even if it is as long as twenty-five years.

If the schedule is being done for the first time, give managers some latitude here; you want them to get used to the concept of disposing of records. However, keep track of record categories where you suspect the retentions are excessive, and monitor the retrievals of the older records. This can be done through computerized indexing of the records in the records center (see Chapter 6). Then, a year later, when the schedule is up for revision, you can negotiate for shorter retentions, pointing out that the older records have not been accessed.

Legal Value

How long the company needs a record is one issue. How long the government thinks you should keep it is another. There are over 3,000 federal statutes and regulations governing records retention, plus a variety of state and local legislation. And no government or court will accept ignorance of a regulation as a satisfactory excuse for noncompliance.

Some companies simply adopt a suggested or "recommended" retention schedule prepared by a vendor or consultant for general use. While such a schedule may serve as a guideline, you don't want to follow it blindly because different types of companies are accountable to different regulatory agencies. As a result, two companies may have different retention requirements for the same record. Also, state and local requirements vary widely, so your company must comply with the retention requirements for the states in which it does business.

As a further complication, each government agency sets its retention requirements autonomously: One agency may specify a three-year period, another six years, and a third may simply say "maintain the record." Normally you must comply with the longest period set by the agencies that regulate your company, although "maintain the record" may be taken to mean the administrative value.

This may all sound so overwhelming that your reaction is, "Let's keep everything forever. Then we're sure to be in compliance." True, but that is a very costly form of compliance. First, there is the expense of storing the records. Second, if the company is sued, it will be required to produce everything it has relating to the suit, and if everything's been kept, the cost of finding and reproducing all appropriate documents may be substantial. Third, the records you produce may not always be in your best interests. An old document may contain information damaging to the company's case. If you're not required to keep the document and have destroyed it in compliance with your retention policy, you're protected. But if you have it, you must produce it.

So what is the solution? Fortunately, there are now a number of references available. A very good overall treatment of the legal issues involved in records retention is Donald Skupsky's *Recordkeeping Requirements.** This book also includes most of the more common legal requirements.

Skupsky also offers a three-volume loose-leaf publication that contains all federal and state requirements related to records retention and which is updated annually. Another option is the *Guide to Record Retention Requirements*, published annually by

---

* See the References at the end of this book for information on all of the publications mentioned here.

the Office of the Federal Register. This publication summarizes key federal requirements and is available at a nominal cost.

If your company is heavily regulated by a particular agency, it's a good idea to obtain the appropriate title(s) of the federal regulations that regulate your industry and review the retention requirements listed in it. For example, a pharmaceutical company would be interested in Title 21, Food and Drugs, while a stock brokerage firm would be concerned with Title 17, Commodity and Securities Exchange. (The various federal regulations, as well as the *Guide to Record Retention Requirements*, are available from the U.S. Government Printing Office.)

Your next question probably is "Can't I turn all this over to our corporate counsel and let them figure it out?" Possibly, but don't count on it. While some attorneys are quite knowledgeable about records retention, many are not. If you simply hand your legal staff a list of records and ask how long you should keep them, you may wait a very long time for an answer.

A better approach is to do some of the homework yourself. Start with the administrative values requested by your department heads. Then use the publications discussed above to help you review the retentions, and modify them as needed to comply with legal requirements. Record the appropriate legal citation on the inventory form where it says "legal retention."

Your legal staff can then review the proposed retentions and modify them as they feel is appropriate. This expedites matters considerably. But remember: Although you can do the "legwork," it is imperative that your attorneys approve the schedule. If the schedule ever becomes a factor in litigation, whether it was approved by your company's legal department is one of the first issues that will be raised.

Your legal department's input is important for another reason. Attorneys know what types of litigation your organization is likely to be involved in and which records typically need to be produced. Records are a double-edged sword: Sometimes having a record can aid your cause, sometimes it can harm it. For example, keeping records of employee medical tests may prove that an employee was tested in compliance with the law and that no medical problems were revealed. Hence, keeping such records longer than the Occupational Safety and Health Administration (OSHA) requirements might be beneficial. On the other hand, a memo questioning quality control on a product could be detrimental to the company.

Remember, all records are not on paper. While electronic mail, or the practice of sending messages via computer from one individual to another, can eliminate a great deal of "telephone tag," it also creates problems. Depending on your systems procedures, messages may be captured on a system backup and retained for a long period of time.

Suppose while you're out of town you're requested to do something clearly against company policy. When you return, you respond, denying the request. But although the request was captured on a weekly or monthly backup, the response has been erased after receipt. A records search required by litigation that reveals the request but not the response could be quite damaging.

Also, people tend to communicate informally via electronic mail—much as they talk on the telephone. One company's search of electronic mail messages that had been captured on backups revealed not only items that could be misinterpreted but also frivolous and X-rated communications. While these may not have caused the company to lose a court case, they certainly didn't enhance its image.

In response to this problem, many organizations have adopted a multifaceted approach. First, backups for such directories are maintained for only a very brief period. The changes involved in backup procedures are usually worth the effort. Second, users are educated through training sessions and written communications. Basically, they are taught that electronic mail is not the same as a phone conversation and that professional judgment should be used, just as when writing a letter.

Fiscal/Tax Value

In a typical organization, approximately half the records are financial in nature, and many of these have tax implications. Financial records should be retained for a minimum of the Internal Revenue Service's statutes of limitations (generally three years from the date the return is filed or due, whichever is later). However, some state statutes of limitations for tax records exceed IRS requirements. If you're taxed in one of those states, your retentions must comply with state, not federal, requirements.

In addition to regulations governing paper records, the IRS has specific retention requirements for information on computer-readable media (IRS Revenue Procedure 86-19), which must be complied with.*

Also, if, like virtually all large companies and some smaller ones, your organization is audited annually by the IRS and/or by the state, your tax staff has agreements with these tax agencies as to how long certain records must be retained. These agreements usually specify retention until the audit for a particular year is resolved. Your first step here should be to meet with your finance/ tax staff and determine what, if any, agreements exist. In many cases, the retention for tax-related documents may have to be set as after-tax audit (ATA) instead of for a specific number of years.

Archival or Historical Value

Records can also have historical or archival value. You may remember the republishing of an early Sears, Roebuck catalog. Although the information in that catalog no longer had legal, fiscal, or administrative value, it was definitely of historical interest. Similarly, businesses often keep permanent copies of company publications, annual reports, selected advertisements, and photographs of major corporate events. Sometimes a corporate archivist is responsible for maintaining these records. But if there is no archivist, the responsibility usually falls to the records manager.

Setting the Final Retention Value

Normally the retention period on the schedule is the longest of the four values just discussed. And, of course, many records may

---

*Since legal and tax requirements do change frequently, always verify them either through the appropriate agency or through a current reference source.

only have one or two retention values, such as administrative or administrative and legal.

Preparing the Retention Schedule

Your next step is relatively simple—packaging all of the information together in a retention schedule with supporting procedures and other material. If the inventory information and final retention values have already been input into a computer database, generating the schedule is simply a matter of formatting and running a report.

Virtually any standard relational database software can be used for the retention schedule. Or you may want to use a commercial records management software package (see Chapter 6). Almost all of these packages have a separate module for the retention schedule.

I usually include more fields in the database than I actually print out in the schedule. The additional information is of value to the records management staff, although a user of the schedule does not need it to determine if a record should be kept.

Typical database fields are:

- Department name
- Department number
- Record title
- Form or report number
- Description of the record
- Whether or not the record is vital (discussed in Chapter 8)
- The media on which the record is kept
- Office retention
- Retention in storage
- Legal citation for retention, if any
- Comments (a field for any notes you might have, such as, "Consider reducing retention to six years when schedule is revised.")

Exhibit 5-1 is a sample of an entry in a retention database, and Exhibit 5-2 is a sample of a portion of a retention schedule. Usu-

Exhibit 5-1. Sample of Retention Database Entry.

Dept. No.	Record Title	Rpt. No.	Media	Office	Storage
803	Employee attendance report	HR29	PA	3	0
803	Employee handbook		PA	P	0
803	Employment applications—not hired		PA	1	0
803	I-9 immigration forms		PA	AT	3
803	Performance appraisals		PA	3	0
803	Personnel files		PA	AT	6

ally I sort the retention schedule first by department number, then alphabetically by record title. Sorting by department number is the most helpful, since a department can quickly identify the records for which it is responsible and how long it should keep them.

The schedule and supporting materials should all be part of the records manual (see Chapter 14 for a discussion of the entire manual), but here it's appropriate to consider what material is needed to explain and support the retention schedule.

You'll need a discussion on how to use the retention schedule. Here you'll state how the records are organized on the schedule (i.e., by department, then title) and explain any codes or abbreviations used. For example, while most retentions can be given in years, some will be event-driven. Codes for these retentions might include:

AC   After completion, expiration, or settlement, as with projects, contracts, agreements. Thus 1AC refers to one year after completion.

Exhibit 5-2.   Sample Retention Schedule Form.

Dept. No.:	345
Dept. Name:	Accounts payable
Record Title:	Invoices - Vendor - Paid
Description:	Invoice, purchase order, purchase requisition, receiving report, and check copy. Filed by vendor number.
Vital:	No
Media:	PA {paper}
Office:	1 yr.
Storage:	ATA {after-tax audit}
Legal Cit.:	IRS
Comments:	Currently occupies 15 4-drawer lateral cabinets; evaluate for conversion to microfilm or optical disk.

AD	After disposal, as with property and equipment.
AT	After termination (e.g., for employees).
ATA	After-tax audit
P	Permanent (use this one sparingly!).

It's also a good idea to include a discussion of duplicate records and retention practices for the general categories of records that are maintained by a number of different departments. Exhibit 5-3 illustrates an example of a portion of such a discussion.

Exhibit 5-3.   General record categories; duplicate records.

For certain categories of records, duplicates are retained by a number of departments. This list identifies the department responsible for holding the "official" copy or the "copy of record." The record is also listed on that department's retention schedule. This list also gives the maximum time period that another department may hold a duplicate of the record. However, the duplicates are not listed on the retention schedule under each department that might have them.

This list also specifies the retention policy for general categories of records that are originated by a number of different departments, such as various correspondence files.

- *Correspondence and memos.* Keep chronological correspondence files for the current year plus one prior year. The same retention applies to other collections of general or miscellaneous correspondence. Correspondence relating to a particular subject should be filed with that topic and retained for the same period of time. The same guidelines apply to internal memoranda.
- *Financial records.* The accounting department keeps the official copy of the following records:

—Budget reports
—Check requests
—Employee expense reports
—Invoices
—Time cards

Other departments should keep these records for no longer than one year.

Getting the Schedule Approved

The next step in the process is the most critical of all—getting approval for the schedule. Here, if you're not careful, the whole process can come to a screeching halt. I've known of schedules languishing on top managers' desks for over a year waiting for approval. Before discussing how to avoid that pitfall, let's consider who should approve the manual.

Obviously, organizational practice for getting policies and procedures approved varies from company to company. However, as a general rule, I've found the following sequence useful.

1. *Send each department head his or her respective schedule for review.* Because you don't want to follow up on all of these people individually, state in your cover memo that they have two weeks (or whatever time seems appropriate) to review the material and that if you don't hear from them by then, you'll assume they are comfortable with the schedule and will send it on to senior management.

2. *Submit the schedule for a legal and tax review.* Senior management is unlikely to approve it unless they know that the department heads and the legal and tax departments have approved it.

3. *Once you've received the blessing of the legal and tax staff, send the schedule to senior management.* Here corporate practices vary. In some organizations, each vice-president approves the schedule for his or her area; in others, the CEO or even the board of directors also approves the entire schedule.

Often reviewers are hesitant to approve the schedule because they are unsure of their knowledge in this area. Several things will help speed the process.

1. *Be sure they understand how the schedule was prepared and who has already reviewed it.* For example, the legal department needs to know what preliminary steps you have taken, using available resources, to review legal requirements for various records. It's also a good idea to print out the "legal citation" field from the database on the copy you send to legal.

2. *Ask them to set their own deadline for reviewing the material.* People are more likely to meet deadlines they set. This practice also helps you deal with sensitive egos; some people resent your asking them to do something by a particular date. Of course, you'll confirm the deadline in writing with a thank-you note.

3. *A few days before the material is due back, give the reviewers a friendly reminder in the form of a phone call.* Ask if they have any questions so far—much more tactful than asking, "Have you looked at it yet?" If they live on Olympus and don't talk to ordinary mortals, give the reminder to their secretaries.

Usually these approaches work, but if they don't, calculate approximately how many records can be destroyed if the schedule is approved and what the current cost of storing those records is. This statistic usually gets everyone's attention.

A somewhat more drastic, though highly effective, approach is to ask for approval of the schedule at a senior staff meeting. Send out the schedule ahead of time accompanied by memos from the legal and tax departments indicating their approval. At the meeting, ask for immediate approval.

I have used this technique successfully when a schedule had to be approved promptly so records could be destroyed before a forthcoming move. At one company, we asked for approval, and the CEO said, "I reviewed it carefully over the weekend. Looks good to me. Any problems?" Not surprisingly, there were none.

Implementing the Schedule

Getting a policy approved is one thing. Getting it implemented is another. If you simply mail out the schedule with a cover letter, nothing will happen. It's not that people purposely try to sabotage the program, but being busy, the schedule becomes one of those things they'll do when they have time, which is never.

A better approach is to distribute the schedule at training sessions. I usually have two types of sessions. The first is a short one for managers, which emphasizes the rationale behind the program and asks for their cooperation in making sure their areas comply. If possible, I get a representative from legal or senior management to "drop in" and say a few words about the program's importance.

The second type of session is a "nuts and bolts" one for anyone who will be actively involved in implementing the program.

I try to keep the group size small—twenty or fewer is a good guideline. If the group is much larger, people don't ask questions and their minds tend to wander.

In this session, I review all of the procedures for the program: how to use the schedule, how to dispose of the records, how to box records and send them to storage. While all of these procedures are written in the manual, I've found that going over them orally substantially improves compliance.

After the training sessions comes the "file purge." Specific days are set aside for implementing the schedule—a day for reviewing the files and disposing of all records past their retention and a day for boxing the records that should go to storage. This effort should be coordinated with building services—you'll need to have plenty of strong bodies available to haul away the trash and transport the boxes to storage.

If properly presented and promoted, this event can be a rather enjoyable break from routine activities. Many companies allow employees to dress more casually on these days; some order in pizza or provide snacks. Keep track of how many records are disposed of and how many boxes go to storage—you'll be surprised at the results. You may also want to take some photographs or have the event featured in the company newsletter.

Updating the Schedule

Records retention is an ongoing process. When a schedule is never revised, people begin to distrust it. They suspect, quite rightly, that the standards set five or ten years ago are no longer appropriate, and they start disregarding it.

Each year the records coordinators should review the entries for their departments with all appropriate personnel within the department. Record categories that are no longer maintained should be dropped from the schedule and new ones added as necessary. Finally, retentions for existing records should be reviewed to see if they are still appropriate.

As records manager, it is your responsibility to check current legal sources to see if any legal requirements have been added or changed. Then make sure that all changes to the schedule are reviewed and approved by appropriate management personnel, including your legal and tax departments.

After the schedule is revised, it's a good idea to have training sessions for any new personnel who may have joined the company since the last series of sessions.

The final step in the process is the file purge. Making this an annual event does a great deal to ensure compliance with the program. Scheduling it approximately three to five months after year-end usually works well. Holding it immediately after year-end means records created near the end of the year may still be active. If they're sent to storage, they often need to be retrieved almost immediately. Waiting a few months eliminates this problem.

Of course, a department need not wait for file purge days to send its inactive records to storage or to destroy records past their retention. But you'll find overall compliance with the retention schedule much higher if special days are set aside to houseclean the files.

Acquisitions

Even the best records management programs can go into a tailspin when confronted with an acquisition. When your organization acquires another company, it may end up with the acquiree's records as well. I've known records managers suddenly to find out they now have 20,000 more boxes of inactive records than they had the day before. I talk about coping with the boxes in Chapter 6, but let's address modifying the retention schedule now.

The acquired company may have a retention schedule, but don't count on it. And even if it does, the schedule is probably inconsistent with yours in some key areas. In this case, you have two alternatives: to convert the acquired company to your schedule, adding new categories as necessary, or to develop a schedule for the acquiree that is separate from but consistent with yours. The latter approach is usually taken when the acquired company remains a separate entity, at its own place of business, with its own staff.

Typical Results

Implementing a comprehensive records retention program will free up significant amounts of office space. Consider the following statistics from an ARMA survey of companies implementing a records retention schedule for the first time. On average, 24.1 percent of the total volume of a company's records are destroyed when a retention program is begun; 32.3 percent are sent to inactive storage at a records center; only 43.6 percent of the records remain in the office area. In other words, over half the office space occupied by records is now available for other uses.

6

The Records Center
Storage Options—Indexing
Records in Storage

In records management, the term *records center* is used to indicate a central storage area for the company's inactive records—records that must be kept but are not used enough to justify high-cost office storage. Although some companies use the term to indicate a central file room for active records, that usage tends to create confusion. Likewise, the term *company archives* to refer to the inactive records storage area is a misnomer. In reality, an archives is a special storage area for the permanent preservation of documents of historic significance.

Because they are designed for inactive records, records centers should provide cheap storage while permitting relatively prompt retrieval. Meeting these dual objectives means that records centers are visually unexciting—even ugly—and totally functional.

Records Center Alternatives

You have three basic alternatives for storing inactive records: (1) an on-site records center; (2) an off-site facility operated by the company; or (3) a commercial records center. Let's examine the pros and cons of each option.

The On-Site Records Center

Storing inactive records on-site is a common practice for companies (often small to medium-size) that have available space within their buildings. Usually such companies own their buildings and are located in areas with comparatively inexpensive real estate. While it would hardly be economical to rent office space in midtown Manhattan to store inactive records, if your company should own a building in Dubuque, Iowa, with space to spare, an on-site center might be your best option.

An on-site center is often located in the basement or on the ground floor so that the weight of the records does not strain the building unduly. Also transferring records in and out of the building is simplified because elevators are not involved. An on-site records center should have adequate fire protection, security, and lighting, as well as all the other physical characteristics of records centers that are discussed later in this chapter. The on-site center is *not* a large storeroom for departmental Christmas decorations or other infrequently used items. It should be used only for records.

The Off-Site Company-Operated Facility

Large organizations often build or lease totally separate buildings for use as a records center. This approach is viable for a company with a very large amount of inactive records. Other organizations segregate a portion of an existing warehouse and establish an off-site records center there. This approach would be feasible if your company already had one or more warehouses (possibly used to store products).

Such space is usually less expensive than space in the company's office buildings, yet it allows the company to maintain direct control of its own records. Key considerations here are the accessibility of the warehouse and what provisions will be made for transporting needed records to the office building(s).

The Commercial Records Center

Your third alternative is to use a commercial records center. This type of facility is designed exclusively for records storage and provides a wide range of services, including the retrieval and destruction of records at your request.

If your company does not have available storage space, using a commercial facility may be the only option. Some companies with available space still opt to use a commercial facility because they don't want to incur the capital expenditures needed for an in-house facility or to maintain the staff necessary to support it.

There's no easy way to tell whether an in-house operation is cheaper. If low-cost storage space is available, an in-house operation is usually cheaper in the long run. However, *long run* may mean a payback of five, seven, or nine years, and many companies require a quicker return on capital investments.

Of course, financial considerations are not the only ones. Some organizations opt for in-house facilities because they don't want company records to leave company premises; or an out-of-the-way location simply may not have access to a reliable commercial vendor. Others opt for commercial centers because they require less effort than managing an in-house facility.

Selecting a Commercial Records Center

If you decide to use a commercial facility, the decision should be made carefully. Despite the many very reputable, highly professional facilities, some less-than-desirable operations do exist.

First determine what services you need and make sure the facilities under consideration can provide them.

• *Media to be stored.* Some vendors store only paper records, some only microfilm and magnetic media, and others all types of media. Microfilm and magnetic media need a climate-controlled facility with constant temperature and humidity. Many facilities have special vaults for film and magnetic media and use regular warehouse space for paper.

• *Computer indexing of your records.* A steadily increasing number of vendors provide computerized indexing. This is a highly desirable feature and well worth the cost. As part of such a system, the vendor should be able to provide you with a monthly printout listing which cartons are due for destruction (based on retention data you supply). The vendor should also be able to generate index listings by department so that each department can have a printout of its holdings. Likewise, the vendor should be able to break your monthly invoice down by department so you can internally charge each department back for the storage costs it incurs.

Some systems are sophisticated enough for you to access your records index by modem. While you cannot change any of the data in the system, you can view your holdings at any time. This eliminates the need for monthly printouts and also lets you verify when data have been entered into the system.

A few cautions here: Be sure you and the vendor agree in advance, in writing, as to exactly what level of indexing will be done; also reach agreement as to how long it will take between when the records are received and when they are input into the computer; finally, make sure the vendor backs up the index regularly and stores the backup in another location. Yes, I know this sounds incredibly obvious, but I know of a case where the vendor did not back up the index, "lost" the entire database, and had to re-create it manually. It took months!

• *Pickup service.* Most vendors provide pickup and delivery service for a fee. Usually records are picked up the next day, but find out in advance what the vendor's practice is and when delays might occur.

• *Retrieval of records.* You usually have several choices in terms of retrieval. Normal service is next-day delivery of the requested record. "Rush" delivery (usually within two hours) is available at a substantially higher cost. But now an increasing number of vendors will fax the record to you—an attractive alternative (if it's only a few pages), since you get the record quickly and for comparatively little cost.

Do you want the vendor to send you the entire box or just

pull a specific file or pages from a file out of the box? Most vendors will do it either way, provided your boxes are in good order.

Also learn the procedure for requesting a record after normal working hours or during a weekend. This service is especially important if you store magnetic media.

• *On-site client work area.* When someone from your company needs to browse through a number of boxes of records, possibly as part of an audit or in response to litigation, it's much easier to send one or more staff people to the records center than to send hundreds of boxes to your office. Many commercial centers have an audit room available for clients to use for such searches.

• *Destruction of records.* Most facilities will handle the destruction of records past their retention upon receipt of a written authorization from a designated individual at your firm. For an extra charge, they will shred the records and certify the confidentiality of the destruction.

Of course, level of service should not be your only consideration in selecting a commercial records storage facility. There are several other issues. For example:

• *The physical facility.* Be sure to visit any facility you are seriously considering. The pictures in the brochure sometimes bear little relation to reality. While records centers are not glamorous, the facility should be neat and orderly. The building itself should be fire-resistant. The paper records storage area should be sprinklered, while the storage area for microfilm and magnetic media should have a chemical fire extinguishing system. The facility should have both fire and security alarms with direct tie-ins to the fire department and police department.

Yes, I did say sprinklered. The water damage from sprinklers going off (and they only go off where the fire is) is far less than the damage from either an uncontrolled fire or the fire department hoses. The National Fire Protection Association (NFPA) has a standard for the protection of records (ANSI/NFPA 232) and a manual for fire protection for archives and records centers

(ANSI/NFPA 232AM).* NFPA 232AM specifically addresses fire protection in large records storage facilities, and any vendor you consider should be in compliance with it as well as will the community's own building codes and regulations.

• *Staffing.* Find out whom you will be dealing with on a regular basis (usually not the person who sells you the service). Do you feel comfortable with their level of expertise and attitude? How available are they? Who is the backup in their absence? Also find out if security checks are made on all personnel working at the center and if employees are bonded.

• *References.* In addition to checking the references provided by the center (which, of course, will be positive), use your ARMA contacts. Ask other records managers in the area whom they use and their level of satisfaction. When I visit a commercial records center, I always make a mental note of which company names are on the various boxes in storage and contact one or two that were not given as references.

Also find out if the firm is a member of the Association of Commercial Records Centers (ACRC)—the professional group for these businesses. While belonging is not an absolute guarantee of quality, members are required to subscribe to a code of ethics and most reputable firms are members. The Association can provide you with the names of members in your area (see the Resource list at the back of the book for the Association's address).

• *Cost.* Comparing prices of the various records centers is always a bit of a challenge. You pay a separate charge for each activity they perform, e.g., shelving, indexing, storage, retrieval, or destruction. And you'll find one center will be lower on one item and higher on another. What I do is quantify what a company's annual usage is likely to be (i.e., how many boxes going in, going out, being stored, being retrieved) and cost out each center under that scenario.

Two charges deserve special attention. The first is cartons. Does the center require you to use its cartons and, if so, are they

---

*See References under *Protection of Records* (ANSI/NFPA 232) and *Fire Protection for Archives and Records Centers* (ANSI/NFPA 232AM).

competitively priced? Some centers charge considerably more for the cartons than you would pay if you bought them directly from a carton vendor. While I don't believe a center should require you to use its cartons, it is fair for it to require you to use cartons of a certain quality and size. If you send over records in old copier paper cartons and the bottoms fall out when their people pick up the boxes, they'll understandably be aggrieved. And since the shelving is designed to handle boxes of a particular size, odd-size boxes don't use space efficiently and may not fit on the shelves.

The second charge to watch for is the cost of permanently removing your records. Some centers have a very high charge (usually approximately one year's storage for a box). This charge is designed to make it difficult for you to cost-justify removing your records, even though you are unhappy with the center's service. However, if you're already using a center with a high permanent removal fee and are dissatisfied, don't despair. Often another center will agree to pay the removal fee if you decide to move your records to its facility.

If you do your homework, you should be able to find a quality commercial operation that will meet your needs well. Now let's consider the other option: establishing your own records center.

Records Center Design

Both company-operated and commercial records centers tend to be remarkably similar in physical design. Moreover, the design guidelines have changed relatively little in the past twenty-five years for a simple reason: No one has found a better way.

Off-site company records centers generally are single-level concrete structures with windows limited to office and entry areas. Such a structure provides good security and fire protection. The building's ceiling is generally at least fifteen feet high to allow maximum use of space through shelving tiers and stacked cartons. Obviously, an on-site center will probably have a lower ceiling and the storage area may not be windowless.

In addition to an area for records storage, the center should have adequate office space for its staff as well as work areas for center users. Just as in a commercial center, individuals may need to browse through one or more cartons. Having a work area means the cartons don't have to leave the center and allows users to request other cartons easily.

When microfilm, magnetic media, videotapes, or audiotapes are stored in the center, temperature and humidity should be strictly controlled. Otherwise, if the climate permits, a good ventilation and heating system may suffice. In any case, the offices and work areas should be air-conditioned for the comfort of their users.

As we've already discussed, good fire protection is essential. The center should comply with the NFPA standards discussed earlier. Smoking should be prohibited in the records storage areas. And while, for security reasons, there may be only one entrance to the records center, there should be other fire exits. Emergency procedures should be reviewed carefully with all center employees, and fire drills must be conducted regularly.

Although fire is the most obvious danger, records centers do have the potential for a variety of accidents. Pulpit-type ladders (i.e., ladders with platforms for holding cartons) should be used. All staff should be trained in proper lifting procedures to avoid back injuries, and job descriptions should specify what weight the individuals should be able to lift regularly (usually 40 or 50 pounds). This latter requirement is not sex discrimination; it's bad back, slipped-disk discrimination. Be sure that all shelving is properly installed by a reliable contractor. In at least one records center, the collapse of poorly installed shelving has resulted in a death. Have your safety manager or OSHA expert, if you have one, inspect the center and make appropriate recommendations.

The records center should have both phone and facsimile service. Facsimile is especially helpful if the center is off-site. Good lighting is also important. Obviously, the shelving should not be installed directly under the light fixtures, thus blocking the light. Again, this has happened more than once. If possible, the lighting system should be wired so that the lights in each aisle and/or section can be turned on and off separately to conserve energy.

Cartons and Shelving

For the actual storage of paper records, a combination of standard-size cartons and steel shelving will keep costs down, use space efficiently, and permit quick retrieval. For these reasons, most records centers use a system similar or identical to the one outlined below and shown in the photograph.

The standard storage container is made of double-wall, 200-pound corrugated cardboard with handholds for ease in carrying. The carton is 15 inches long, 12 inches wide, and 10 inches high. This versatile container can hold legal-size files along the 15-inch length and letter-size files along the 12-inch width. When removed from their binders, computer printouts can lie flat in the carton. These containers can be stored flat when not in use to reduce storage space and are assembled easily.

I would avoid the longer 24- and 30-inch boxes. They do not hold up as well because they are so heavy. The weight also makes them unwieldy for office staff to load and handle. Indexing records is more of a problem, too. Because of their greater capacity, you're more likely to end up with several different types of records in a box, which complicates indexing, retrieval, and destruction of the records.

You have a choice as to lids. I prefer the shoebox-style lift-off lid, as it makes searching for records in the box easier. However, some records managers feel the single-unit box with a foldover lid eliminates lost lids. (Personally, I think lids procreate! It seems as if every time a major reboxing is completed, a surplus of lids results.)

I recommend that you avoid the combination corrugated and steel pull-out file units that are stacked on top of each other. Some users experience difficulty in opening drawers near the bottom of the stack and find that the units do not wear well. Also these units are costly, are difficult to transport, and require more aisle space than cartons stacked on shelving.

A commercial records center.

Courtesy of Commercial Archives.

The shelving itself may be steel, particleboard, or plywood, while the uprights are, of course, steel. Steel shelving is the most durable, but also the most costly. The shelving units are usually 42 inches wide and 30 inches deep, with 23 inches between shelves. Each shelf holds twelve cartons (three across, two deep, and two high). To conserve space further, two shelving units may be fastened together along the 42-inch width. Thus, to get to an inner box, a maximum of three boxes would be moved.

Usually the aisles between the rows of shelves are 30 to 36 inches wide. The main "feeder" aisles are 4 to 6 feet wide, depending on the type of equipment (e.g., forklift truck, handcart) that must pass down them.

Organizing the Records

To use available space most effectively, don't segregate records by department. Instead place the cartons in any available space and assign box numbers to denote the locations. (Of course, you wouldn't mix more than one department's records within a box.) To retrieve a particular carton, the center staff simply checks the index to determine the box number and then locates the record accordingly.

While you are not grouping boxes by department, there are some practical considerations in shelving cartons to keep in mind. Some box locations are less accessible than others. For example, if you butt shelving units together, the boxes in the inner core will be less accessible. Also, boxes on both the bottom and the very highest shelves are harder to access. You may want to shelve boxes with low retrieval needs and long retentions in these areas.

Assigning Box Numbers

The best practice is to assign two numbers to each box. The first number is the location number. You might consider this the box's "street address," as this number tells you where to find the box. I normally use a three-part numbering system. The first number identifies the row the box is on, the second number the shelving unit, and the third number the box's location on that shelving unit. For example, 5-3-36 would mean row 5, shelving unit 3, box 36. Since there are twelve boxes to a shelf, box 36 would be on the third shelf up from the bottom. Or you might prefer to identify the rows by letters of the alphabet, making the box E-3-36.

Since location numbers will be reused if a box is destroyed, it's a good practice to also assign each box a control number. This number might be considered the box's "Social Security number," as it will not be reused. It may be either computer-generated or printed in advance on the records transfer forms (much as check numbers are printed on checks). It could be simply a consecutively issued number (000001, 000002, . . .) or based on the year (91-0001, 91-0002, . . .).

Indexing the Records

An index is essential for the successful operation of any records center. Users should not have to supply box numbers when they request a record, and you should know from the index exactly what boxes you have in the center and where they are located.

Regardless of the size of your records center, I would strongly advocate computerizing the index. An automated index speeds retrieval, reduces records center staff labor, and improves your control over the records in the center. Also the sooner you automate, the easier the process will be. Having worked with conversions of different size facilities, I can assure you it's much easier to convert 3,000 boxes to an automated system than 43,000.

Once the decision is made to computerize the index, a whole string of other decisions must follow. One of the first is what level of detail the index should address. Do you want to index every document, every file in a box, or just the box's overall contents? Most organizations primarily index the overall contents of the box, as the amount of data entry involved in indexing every file or document is significant. If the records are in the box in a specific order, finding a particular file is not difficult. For example, if the 1990 paid invoices are boxed in order of vendor number and the box contains vendors 19381 to 19492, it's easy to locate 19451.

Of course, sometimes it's desirable to index each file or document separately. A hospital sending inactive patient files to storage might want to index each file by patient number. Most computerized systems can be designed to accommodate either approach.

Choosing the Right Hardware and Software

Another set of decisions involves hardware and software. The number of boxes in storage and the amount of information you want to capture on each will affect the hardware. However, with the steadily increasing capacity of hard drives on personal computers, most company-operated records centers find a PC-based system quite satisfactory. It's best to discuss your needs with the systems department and see what approach it recommends and how long implementation will take. Many records managers I know go with a PC-based system because, while it would take three years of prayer and fasting to get the application on the main computer system, it can be up and running on a PC in a few months.

Your first step when selecting software is to decide whether you want a commercial package or an internally developed system. Many of the commercial packages on the market now are designed to run on a personal computer, although some can be upgraded to a larger system. Others are designed solely for a large system.

Several considerations should affect your decision:

• *Can the commercial package meet all your needs?* Before evaluating packages, identify what you want the system to do. Then see how well each package meets that list of objectives.

• *What is the vendor's track record?* How long has the company been in business? How many systems has it installed? What kind of training and support will it provide your staff? How heavily dependent on its support will you be?

• *How do the cost, level of support, and quality compare with an internally developed system?* This is the ultimate question, and I've found the answer varies from organization to organization. Prices on commercial packages are coming down, and access to in-house programming staff is difficult at some companies. On the other hand, I've also seen in-house staff put together a very satisfactory program at a fraction of the cost of a commercial package. You're the best judge of which way to go.

System Specifications

To make these decisions in an intelligent manner, you need to identify exactly what you want the system to do. A records center indexing system is basically a moderately sophisticated relational database. If you are developing the system internally, don't use a spreadsheet or word processing package. Neither one will meet your needs adequately. A functional system can be developed using most standard types of database software. If you elect this approach, select the database software you and your systems staff are most comfortable with.

The primary database for the system will create a record for each box in storage. Typical fields would be:

- *Department name.*
- *Department number.*
- *Record title.*
- *Date from.*
- *Date to.* Two date fields are preferable to one that gives just the year, as some records will be in chronological sequence.
- *Sequence from.*
- *Sequence to.* These fields are useful when you just need to give a summary of the contents, e.g., purchase orders 07895 to 08963.
- *Contents listing.* This would permit a more detailed listing of contents.
- *Destruction date.* If your retention schedule database is linked to the index database, the system should have the ability to calculate destruction dates for you.
- *Date record received at records center.*
- *Contact name.* Whom to call if there's a question; this is especially helpful in large organizations.
- *Control box number.* Either computer-generated or entered from the records transfer form.
- *Locational box number.*

- *Comments.* Useful if you need to annotate the entry, e.g., "box held for litigation; do not destroy."
- *Date destroyed.*
- *Destruction certified by.*

Whether you select a commercial package or develop a system internally, several features are desirable. First, the records management staff should handle all data entry and be able to run both routine and ad hoc reports without assistance. If you decide to let other departments access the database, they should be able to view their own holdings only, not those of other departments, and they should not be able to change any information in the system.

You also want to be able to make global changes to database fields. For example, if a department number changes from 289 to 293, you don't want to have to change each entry manually. It also should be easy to copy repetitive information from record to record. Thus, if there are 350 boxes of 1990 invoices to enter, you don't want to have to key in "invoices" and the date 350 times.

Consider both the frequent and infrequent user of the system. Menu-driven systems with lots of user aids are very helpful for someone who references the database infrequently. On the other hand, the people who enter all the data and know the system very thoroughly shouldn't have to go through three sets of menus every time they need to use the system. Hitting a couple of keys should be all they need to get where they want.

After a box has been destroyed, you may want to transfer the record to a secondary or archival database or run a printout of all destroyed boxes. It is a good practice to keep a record of what has been destroyed in case a destroyed record is requested for litigation. Then you have proof that the record was destroyed as part of your standard records retention policy.

Another desirable feature for the computerized index is the ability to track records that have been checked out to users. This subsystem would typically include:

- Name of individual checking out the record
- Department
- Telephone
- Box/file checked out

- Date checked out
- Date due back
- Date actually returned
- Comments

This subsystem should also allow you to monitor how many times a record has been checked out. This information is very helpful in determining if retention periods should be shortened because a particular record category is not being referenced.

System Reports

One major benefit of a computerized system is the ready access you have to a great deal of information about the records in storage. While the number of reports you can generate is virtually limitless, you'll find these especially helpful:

- *Records due for destruction.* A listing of the records due to be destroyed, sorted by department.
- *Box activity report.* A listing of which boxes have been retrieved and how often.
- *Department listing.* A report listing records in storage by department.
- *Charge-out report.* A listing of boxes or files that have been checked out and not returned.
- *Summary report.* How many boxes have been added to storage, how many destroyed, and total number of boxes now in storage. Data should be listed by department and totaled for the entire organization.
- *Locations available.* A listing of box locations available for new records.

Manual Indexing Systems

While I don't recommend a manual system, it is better than no system at all. In some cases, due to no access to a computer or very limited resources, it may be your only alternative for the short run.

Exhibit 6-1.   Sample Records Center Index Card.

Record Title								Dept. Received From		
Date Received	Received By	Box Number	Contents					Date To Be Destroyed	Date Destroyed	Certified By
			Alpha. or Num.		Date					
			From	To	From	To				

There are two basic ways to set up a manual system. In one, you use an index card similar to the one shown in Exhibit 6-1. A separate card is established for each record title in storage. Each new box received is entered on the card. While this system does not provide as much information as its automated counterpart, it is a simple way to locate records.

With the index card system, you'll also need a separate destruction log. When records are added to the index card, their box numbers are entered in the log under the appropriate month and year for destruction, such as January 1995. Each month, the log is checked and the appropriate departments notified of the pending destructions. When the records are destroyed, that information is recorded on the index card.

The alternative manual system uses a multipart records transfer form (one form per box). One copy of the form is filed under the department responsible for the records, and another copy is filed under the destruction date. This system eliminates the index cards and destruction log. However, you do have the risk of misfiled or misplaced forms—a not infrequent problem if you're dealing with thousands of forms.

7

The Records Center
Operating Procedures

In addition to a comprehensive indexing system, the records center needs simple, effective procedures for transferring records into storage, retrieving them when needed, and destroying them on schedule. Let's consider the transfer process first.

Transferring Records to the Center

The first steps in the transfer process are the responsibility of the departments whose records will be stored. Each department requests the required number of boxes from the records center or supply room. A box holds approximately 14 inches of letter-size files or 11 inches of legal-size files, so calculating the appropriate number of boxes is a simple matter.

Department personnel then assemble the boxes and fill them. Records should be left in their manila file folders and loaded in the box just as in a file drawer. This way, the tops of the folders are clearly visible, and retrieval is simplified. However, records in hanging file folders should be transferred to manila folders. Hanging folders do not fit properly in the cartons, cost too much to go into storage, and take up too much space. Records in binders should be removed from the binders, as binders take up too much space and can be reused. Fastening bundles of records together with rubber bands is not a good idea. The bands will break after a year or so, and then you have masses of loose paper to grapple with.

Make sure users understand that all records in a box must have the same destruction date and, if possible, belong to the same record category. One of the biggest reasons for misplaced records is that someone has a couple of inches of space left in a box and throws in an odd few files to fill it out. The files aren't indexed and are lost forever. For that reason, I usually suggest that as long as a box is at least two-thirds full, it be accepted—a little empty space is much less of a problem than lost files. Along the same lines, discourage people from stuffing the box as fully as possible. Overloaded cartons do not hold up well.

After the boxes are filled, the department completes a records transfer form for each box (see Exhibit 7-1). The user keeps one copy of the form as a control, until the records center acknowledges receipt of the box. Another copy serves as a data entry form for the records center. The third copy may be either a self-adhesive label affixed to the end of the box or a nonadhesive version placed inside.

There are two schools of thought on labeling cartons. You can put a descriptive label on the end of the box so you can readily see what's inside. Or you can place only the box location number and control number on the label. This improves security, since an unauthorized person who has gained access to the records center cannot tell what's in the box. But if you do adopt this second approach, be sure to put a copy of the form inside the box. That way, if the ultimate disaster occurs and the box is not indexed or is accidentally removed from the index, you can still identify its contents.

Also write the location and control numbers in indelible felt-tip marker on the other end of the box. I realize this is like wearing a belt and suspenders, but I've known of cases where defective adhesive caused labels to come off.

When the boxes reach the records center, first make sure you have received all of them. Your staff may not be able to index the boxes that day, but the later you discover that a carton is lost, the

Exhibit 7-1.   Sample Records Transfer Form.

RECORDS TRANSFER FORM

96752

Dept. Name	Dept. No.
Record Title (as listed on the retention schedule)	
Date From	Date To
Filing Sequence/Contents Description	
Date Sent to Center	Destruction Date
Form Prepared By	
Approval of Records Coordinator	

═══════════════════════════════════

Box Location (to be completed by records center)

more difficult it will be to locate it. The department can either assign temporary numbers to each box (1 of 20, 2 of 20, . . .) to aid in the verification process or submit a transfer summary, a form listing all boxes in the shipment.

Next verify that the boxes belong in storage. If the records are not listed on the retention schedule for storage, you'll need to determine if they should be added. Occasionally a record category that was overlooked in the inventory has a legitimate need for retention. But, in most cases, the records don't belong in the records center either because long-term retention is unnecessary or because they are duplicates of what another department stores. In these situations, notify the department and tell it that you can't accept the records; if they are past their retention, offer to destroy them.

Also be sure that the destruction date is in compliance with the retention schedule. If the date is incorrect, correct it and contact the records coordinator for that area to explain why.

After the boxes are indexed, notify the department that they have been received and shelved. If you're using a computerized indexing system, simply send the department a printout of the index entry for each box. This way the department can verify your data entry. If you have a manual system, send the department a copy of the transfer form with the box's location written on it. Although departments don't retrieve records themselves, their comfort level will be considerably higher if they know where their boxes are.

Retrieving Records From Storage

The key to user confidence in the records center is having an effective retrieval process. Normally, users should be able to request a record by phone, electronic mail, facsimile, or interdepartmental mail.

A key consideration in the retrieval process is deciding what to check out to a user—the entire box or just an individual file or record? My personal preference is to check out the file or document. When an entire box is checked out, files may be removed and never replaced. Also, if anyone else needs a record from the box, you'll have to retrieve it from the current user.

Checking out specific records is especially important when records in a box might be needed by a number of different users. For example, a bank's paid-off mortgage files might be retrieved by several different departments. If one department has a box, other departments' access to mortgages in that box is slowed down significantly.

Of course, there are exceptions to the practice of checking out specific files. Personnel and payroll records are often delivered to the records center in cartons that are taped shut because access to the files is limited to those departments. Boxes with highly confidential records such as these should go to the department unopened.

The issue of access is not limited to personnel or payroll records. You need a policy on who may retrieve what records from the records center. While records such as the paid-off mortgages might be available to several departments, in general, the department sending the records to storage should be the only one able to retrieve them directly. If another department needs the record, it would need permission from the department accountable for it. For example, the marketing department would need authorization from accounts payable to obtain a copy of an old invoice. You may also want to specify who in a department may retrieve records—perhaps only the department head and a designated backup.

If you're using a commercial records center, all retrievals should be cleared through the records management department. Give the center a list of the three or four individuals who are authorized to request records retrieval, and make sure all requests go through them. This protects both you and the records center from unauthorized retrievals.

Commercial centers provide you with a procedure and form to use when requesting records. If you establish an in-house records center, you'll need a form similar to the one in Exhibit 7-2. This form is basically self-explanatory, with the exception of the "remarks" space at the bottom. Here records center personnel can indicate if they had any difficulty locating the record, if the re-

Exhibit 7-2.   Records Request.

RECORDS REQUEST	
To be completed by requesting department. Send all copies to Records Center	
Record Title	Dept. Requesting
Record Date	Send To
Box No. (Not Required)	Phone No.
Record Detail	
To be completed by Records Center.	
Requested by: ☐ Phone ☐ Messenger ☐ Mail ☐ Visit	Sent by: ☐ Mail ☐ Messenger ☐ Visit
Searched by	Time Spent
Date Due	Date Returned
Refiled by	
Remarks	
Copy 1: Tickler File Copy 3: On Out Card Copy 2: On Record	

quester supplied incorrect information, or if the record could not be found.

You'll need a three-part form if the charge-out system is computerized, a four-part one if it's not. The user keeps one copy as a control until the record is received. Another copy is attached to the record, thus identifying it for the user. The third copy is attached to an OUT card placed in the box, which expedites refiling and also lets you know what files are out of a box.

If the indexing system is manual, the fourth copy is placed in a tickler file under the date the record is due back in the center. A two- or three-week checkout period is common, but I prefer two weeks because requesters are less likely to misplace records in the shorter time frame. If the record is not returned by the due date, a records center staff member contacts the user to determine if he or she still needs the record. If the charge-out system is computerized, the follow-up can be computer-generated.

Follow-up procedures are essential if the integrity of the records in the center is to be preserved. Without such procedures, users often forget to return records, which then become lost or misplaced.

If you are using a manual follow-up system, save the tickler file copies for the year, filing them by record title. Then at the end of the year, you'll be able to identify which record categories were accessed during the year. As discussed earlier, this can be valuable information for determining which retention periods to shorten.

From a user's standpoint, timely delivery of records is critical. Determine what time frame you can realistically meet and commit yourself to it. If your records center is staffed all day, how long will it take to retrieve a record and deliver it to the user through the interdepartmental mail service? If yours is a small center that does not require full-time staffing, you may want to tell users that "if we receive your request by 10 A.M., you'll receive the record by 2 P.M." or use some similar approach. This system makes it easier for you to group retrievals together, although, of course, if there's an emergency, someone will need to make a special trip to the records center.

Sometimes, even in the best-managed records centers, a record cannot be found. When this situation occurs, return one copy of the form to the requester. In the "remarks" section, explain what steps were taken to search for the record.

Keep track of what records were not located, as this is an important indicator of the center's efficiency. The formula to use is:

$$\frac{\text{Number of records not found}}{\text{Number of records searched for}} = x\%$$

Calculate this ratio as a percentage. If it is .5 percent or less, your center is doing an excellent job of locating records. If it's over 3 percent, you have a problem.

To determine the cause of the problem, you'll need to analyze some information about the records that were not found. If most of the records not found were requested by a particular department, investigate that department's record-keeping practices. Perhaps its records were not complete when sent to the center, or perhaps its filing procedures are faulty.

If most of the missing records were searched for by the same individual in the records center, he or she may not be diligent enough. For example, if the file is not under the year it was supposed to be, were the years before and after checked? If it's a file on an individual, were other spellings of the name checked? And so on. Retrieval can be a good test of one's detective skills.

Destruction of Records

An important part of the records center's responsibilities is the destruction of records whose retention period has expired. When a department's records are due for destruction, notify the appropriate department head with a memo similar to this:

> The following records are due for destruction in accordance with our company's retention schedule. Please notify us by [*date thirty days later*] of any records that should not be destroyed and the reason why. If I do not hear from you by [*same date*], the records will be destroyed.

Since destroying the records is simply complying with company policy, you don't need a departmental signature to authorize destruction. If records are not to be destroyed, that is a deviation from the policy and a legitimate reason should be supplied—for example, the record is needed for litigation or for an audit.

Since department heads are not always aware of a pending lawsuit or audit, it's a prudent practice to send the legal and tax departments a list of all records due for destruction. As in the case of department heads, destruction will proceed on schedule unless you are notified to the contrary within thirty days.

Confidential records must be disposed of in a manner that prevents their reconstruction. Some recyclers accept sealed cartons and pulp them as is. This option, if available, is the most desirable one. Of course, nonconfidential wastepaper should be recycled whenever possible.

If confidential recycling isn't available, shredding the records is the next best alternative. Shredders are available in a wide range of models, from small units that fit on top of wastebaskets to heavy-duty industrial models. The narrower the shred, the more difficult the reconstruction of the records. Crosscut shredders (units that cut the paper in both directions) make reconstruction virtually impossible, although the shredding process is considerably slower than with straightcut shredders. Remember, after the paper is shredded, it can be recycled.

If you don't choose to destroy the confidential records in-house, there are bonded services that will pick up and destroy the records for you. If you use such a service, have your contract specify that a member of your staff or your company's security department can, without advance notice, accompany the vendor from the time the records are picked up until they are destroyed. While most such services are extremely reliable, there are exceptions, and you want to be sure your records are properly destroyed.

If you're wondering whether this concern about records destruction is rather paranoid, let me just say that clients of mine have found people searching through their garbage. These companies are in highly competitive industries—e.g., biotechnology and software development—and there are always people looking for information to give them an edge either competitively or in terms of the company's stock. Also, your files contain a great deal of confidential information about customers and employees. If these individuals' privacy should be violated, they might choose to take legal action against your company.

The secure destruction of records is also an issue in the office. Most of my clients have metal waste bins with locked lids strategically located throughout the company. Paper in need of confidential destruction is inserted in the slots at the top of the containers. Periodically the bins are removed so their contents can be shredded. It's an especially good idea to have such containers located near key photocopying machines. How often have you made a poor-quality copy of a critical document and just thrown it in the wastebasket?

Two methods of destroying confidential records which I normally avoid are incineration and landfills. Unless an elaborate incinerator with air purifiers is used, burning records creates pollution. Also, unless the incineration is very thorough, some records may not be totally destroyed. As far as landfills are concerned, while eventually records decompose, this is a lengthy process, and we already have a problem with waste disposal. Also, the records could be unearthed.

Cost Analysis

As part of our discussion of records center procedures, we've addressed two measures of a records center's quality: the accuracy of the retrieval process and the speed with which records are delivered to the requester. A third measure is the cost-effectiveness of the services provided.

I'm a great believer in charging users back for the cost of records storage. I've found it to be a great motivator for shortening retention periods. If the cost of storing records permanently is in your budget, all too many departments will insist their records are permanent. If the cost is in their budget, they suddenly realize the records may only be needed for three or four years.

As discussed in Chapter 6, a commercial center should be able to break your bill out by department so that you can charge each one back for its storage. If you're operating an in-house center, you'll have to determine your costs. Of course, you should do this even if you aren't charging users back. You need to know what your costs are for storing in-house, and if that is more cost-effective than using a commercial vendor.

Typical expenses for an in-house center are:

- Rent or depreciation on the building
- Depreciation or lease payments on the center equipment
- Staff (be sure to include fringe benefits and any temporary help used during peak periods; if your staff only works at the center part-time, prorate the cost accordingly)
- Cartons and other supplies
- Data processing costs
- Telephone and utilities
- Insurance
- Security
- Transportation if the center is located off-site

After you've totaled up all the costs, subtract any recycling income received by the center to obtain the net operating cost. Since you're not operating a commercial facility, there's no point in developing an elaborate pricing strategy for users. If you simply divide the net operating cost by the number of boxes in storage, you'll come up with an average cost per box per year to charge users. Since one standard-size box is slightly over one cubic foot, this is also approximately your cost per cubic foot.

Keep in mind that your cost to the user includes shelving, indexing, and retrieving the box. Therefore, if your charge is only slightly higher than a commercial center's annual storage fee for a box, you are really less costly.

Coping With an Acquisition

To complete our discussion of records center operations, we need to address two situations that are not of the records manager's making, but which can complicate his or her life enormously. The first of these is an acquisition. As mentioned in Chapter 5, when your company acquires another company, it often acquires its records.

If possible, this situation should be addressed before the records arrive at your company. It's best if personnel from your company go to the acquired firm and supervise the boxing, labeling, and shipping of the records to be transferred. Here's why. If employees of the acquired firm are going to be laid off, they do not usually feel very positive about the acquisition. In such cases, employees have been known to mislabel records and place them in as much disorder as possible. Also, many duplicate and unnecessary items may be boxed and shipped. Cleaning up the mess becomes a costly and time-consuming process for the acquiring company.

Once the records come into your possession, they'll need to be categorized according to your retention schedule whenever possible. You'll probably need assistance in classification from other departments, especially finance (many of the records will undoubtedly be accounting records).

When there is no match with the retention schedule, appropriate department heads at your company, together with tax and legal input, will need to set retentions. You may find that some of the records are already past their retention and can be disposed of.

Keep a separate listing of the records acquired, their disposition, and the reason why. Then, if litigation occurs, your company is protected from the accusation of selective destruction of records.

Bringing Order Out of Disorder

Another problem is inheriting a warehouse, closet, or storage room full of inactive records that are unindexed and in no particular order. This is a common situation when a company has had no formal records management program. Your first step should be to declare a moratorium on any more records going into the area. Don't let the problem get any worse than it already is.

Next physically organize the records by major subject category (i.e., accounting, marketing, human resources). Then contact each department with records in the area and ask them to appoint a team to work with you on the cleanup process. The team should include one or more managers and one or more clerical personnel.

I usually try to begin with the financial records, as that's normally the largest category. Set up a day for the team to come to the records center, and suggest they dress casually. Even the best-run records center is still a warehouse and less than immaculate.

The managers are responsible for reviewing the records, using the retention schedule as a guide, and determining which ones can be disposed of and which must be kept. The clerical staff's job is to rebox the records that must be kept and complete the transfer forms so that the boxes can be entered into the system correctly.

You may find a few surprises as the housecleaning progresses. One records manager discovered a copy of another manager's divorce proceedings! If you do find such personal records, ship them back to the appropriate individual immediately with a polite note saying you're sure they were sent to the records center by mistake.

You'll also probably find a number of records that aren't on the retention schedule—another reason for having a manager from the department present. He or she can evaluate the records and decide whether they need to be kept.

Admittedly, the cleanup process is less than pleasant. However, it is a onetime event, since the new system and index will make it unnecessary in the future. If any department resists assisting you or maintains it doesn't have the time, point out to management what it's costing to store the records. A few photographs of the chaos also help. And if someone absolutely refuses to come to the records, then let the records come to him or her. I did this with one recalcitrant department manager. We started shipping him three boxes a week and refused to accept them back into the records center until they were properly boxed and labeled.

Blow Your Own Horn!

Once the records center is properly organized, have an open house. Seeing the facility will do a great deal to build people's confidence in using the records center. If you have some interesting archival documents, display them; people enjoy seeing old photographs, documents, and other memorabilia. Demonstrate your computerized indexing system if you have one. And pat yourself on the back—it's no small achievement to have developed a first-rate records center.

8

Vital Records—Your Organization's Lifeblood

In the 1950s and early 1960s, when civil defense was a major national concern, many companies developed elaborate strategies for resuming operations after "the bomb" hit. These plans included provisions for protecting records considered vital to the organization's survival. Today, however, most people feel—quite understandably—that if a nuclear holocaust were to occur, their prime concern would be survival, not reopening a business.

Protecting key records from nuclear destruction is probably a futile effort, but there are other very important reasons for establishing a so-called vital records program. Fire is the most obvious. According to a study conducted by the Safe Manufacturers National Association, 43 percent of the businesses that lose their records in a fire either never reopen or fail within six months.

Other, very real natural dangers include earthquakes, floods, tornadoes, hurricanes—and even volcano eruptions. In addition to unavoidable natural calamities, companies are also vulnerable to bombs and other explosive devices, arson, and sabotage by disgruntled employees or angry members of the public.

Consequently, *every* organization—large or small—needs a vital records program to protect essential information from destruction. Small companies may be even more vulnerable than large ones because all their records and operations are often at one site. Large companies are less vulnerable because the destruction of one location will usually not put the company out of business. Also duplicate copies of some vital records are usually kept at more than one site through routine business practices. However, without a vital records program, even the large multi-location company will have its operations severely hampered by a disaster.

Currently, many companies have a false sense of security because they have installed a "disaster recovery" program. While the term *disaster recovery* can be defined many ways, for most businesses, it means a program to get the computer system up and running again after a disaster. As part of such a program, backup copies of all critical computer media are stored off-site and arrangements have been made to use alternative hardware if the company's equipment is destroyed.

Obviously, this is a very important and worthwhile effort. However, not all of the records essential to your operation are found on your computer systems. If your company's disaster recovery program does not include noncomputer-based records, either the program's scope needs to be broadened to include these documents or it needs to be integrated with a vital records program. If no disaster recovery program exists, one needs to be developed in conjunction with a vital records program.

Clearly, this is an area where the records manager and the systems staff must work closely together. In addition, the company needs to consider also the human aspects of a disaster (e.g., notifying employees, assigning responsibilities, dealing with the possibility of injured personnel) as well as its physical aspects (e.g., where to conduct business if the building is destroyed, rebuilding the facility). As you can see, the project can assume enormous proportions.

In this book, though, I focus only on the records manager's role in the process, a role that typically includes coordination with the systems department's disaster recovery plan, protection of vital records not on the computer system, and participation in the development of the overall plan for resuming operations after a disaster.

Getting Management Support

Most records managers find the vital records program to be the toughest sell of all. Companies give lip service to the idea, but they don't want to spend the money needed to implement a program. And, no doubt about it, a vital records program costs money, since key records have to be duplicated and stored off-site. The program's only monetary return occurs if there is a disaster. Then it may save the business!

Your best approach is to sell the program as insurance. Point out that the company wouldn't think of leaving its buildings, equipment, or key personnel uninsured. Critical information can be just as important. Having a vital records program is equivalent to having insurance for that information.

If you continue to encounter resistance, a good time to raise the issue again is after a disaster has occurred. For example, a number of companies in California reconsidered vital records after the last major earthquake. Or if a company in your area recently has had its operations disrupted due to a fire, this may be a good time to remind senior management that "it could happen to us."

What Are Vital Records?

After you've obtained approval for the program, the next step is to define what we mean by the term *vital records*. The quick, superficial definition is "those records needed to resume operations in the event of a disaster." That definition includes most but not all vital records. For example, although employee pension records aren't necessary for resuming operations, they are considered vital because they represent a legal commitment the company has made and must fulfill. So let's expand our definition to include also the following three categories of records needed to protect:

1. The rights of employees and customers
2. The equity of the business's owners (the stockholders,

partners, proprietor, or even—in the case of the government—the public)
3. The organization's legal and financial status

Now we have a comprehensive general definition of vital records. Each different type of organization has to refine this definition further on the basis of its own business. For example, a manufacturing company would consider vital those engineering drawings and specifications necessary to produce its products. A hospital's vital records would include its patients' medical files, and a bank's would include the status of each depositor's account.

Although organizations have these unique needs, certain general categories are usually vital. These include records that are necessary to do the following:

- *Determine receivables* (what customers and others owe the company). This is critical, as a credit and collection problem often occurs after a disaster. Customers hope their records were destroyed and that the company will be unaware of the money owed it.
- *Determine liabilities* (what the company owes to others). Yes, the company's creditors will remind it of its debts, but you want to be sure the reminders are accurate.
- *Identify fixed assets* (the company's land, buildings, plants, and equipment) and determine their value.
- *Identify the locations and amounts of cash and securities owned by the company.*
- *Identify and, when possible, fulfill existing commitments to customers.*
- *Rebuild facilities* (when appropriate).
- *Develop new business.*
- *State salaries and benefits due employees and former employees* (e.g., re pensions, vacations, and insurance).
- *State any other corporate commitments to employees,* such as union contracts.
- *Meet corporate legal and financial requirements.*

- Resume *manufacture* of products and identify the nature and value of inventory (for manufacturing firms).
- Resume *data processing operations.*

As we've discussed, the last item on the list is usually addressed through the disaster recovery program. And, of course, many of the records on the list can be protected through the disaster recovery system (e.g., payroll records).

However, many vital records are not computer-generated. These include:

- *Contracts, leases, license and franchise agreements,* and other such documents where a signature is critical. (Note: selectivity can be used here. A contract for snow removal is probably not vital, but a contract to build a new plant is.)
- *Laboratory notebooks and other research data.* (Some research data will be computer-generated, but handwritten lab notebooks are usually the pivotal documents.)
- *Drawings, such as engineering drawings and blueprints.* (Newer drawings may be on the computer system, but older ones generally are not.)
- *Production specifications and procedures.*
- *Insurance policies.*
- *Articles of incorporation, bylaws, and board minutes.*
- *Patents, trademarks, and copyrights.*
- *Deeds and titles to property.*

Identifying Your Vital Records

Unless your company is a very small mom-and-pop type of business, no one person will have a broad enough knowledge of all records and systems to identify what should be included in the vital records program. You will need a committee to make the identification. It's best if the committee members are on a fairly high level. That's because if you ask a department head which of his or her records are vital, the answer usually is "all of them." The department head views those records as being essential to the department's work—which is not the same as being essential to the company's existence. Hence, a committee approach works best.

Although the exact membership of the committee will vary from company to company, typically it should include:

- The records manager
- Corporate legal counsel
- The controller or other key finance department member
- The individual in the systems area responsible for the disaster recovery program
- The personnel or human resources manager
- The internal auditor
- The security director
- Representatives from key operational areas such as sales/ marketing, operations/production, research, and engineering

The individuals on the committee should (1) be very familiar with their areas and the records in those areas and (2) be willing and able to devote significant amounts of time to the program until its operation. A good approach is to have the committee meet regularly—perhaps every two weeks—until all vital records are identified and a plan for their protection established.

While this task may sound overwhelming, if you have a retention schedule, you've already done much of the legwork. The schedule, since it lists all of the company's records, is a logical starting point.

First, eliminate nonessential records. Next, eliminate records that contain essential data but which can be reconstructed from other records—for example, accounts payable information is kept in several forms, but only one is deemed vital. Finally, reevaluate those records remaining on the list to ensure that they are vital (but *don't forget that the vital records schedule and the disaster recovery program themselves are vital records!*).

Preparing the vital records schedule from the retention schedule ensures that you don't overlook any critical record categories. In screening the records, the committee should ask itself what the company would be unable to do if a particular record did not exist. If it can't perform an essential activity, the record is vital.

Thorough screening is important because protecting records from accidental destruction is costly. To get the maximum benefit from your investment in the program, protect only essential records.

Protecting the Vital Records

After the company's vital records are identified, the committee must select an appropriate way to protect them. Most companies use a combination of strategies, depending on the record category and its normal usage patterns. The goal is to use the simplest, most economical method that fits the circumstances. You have four choices: (1) existing dispersal; (2) planned dispersal; (3) duplicating the record; and (4) protecting the original.

1. *Existing dispersal. Existing dispersal* is the formal title for the vital records protection you already have. As a normal part of doing business, copies of a record are maintained at more than one company location. For example, if a branch office and corporate headquarters both maintain a copy of a record, that record is protected.

As a corollary to existing dispersal within the company, when copies of your organization's vital records are kept by others outside the company, those records may—under certain circumstances—be considered protected. The qualifier here is compatibility. For example, copies of key litigation files kept by an outside law firm that does work for your company would be protected. However, your creditors' copies of records of the company's liabilities would provide no protection, as their interests are not the same as yours. I would also be leery of assuming that a record filed with a government agency is protected. I've known of too many instances where the agency either could not or would not provide a copy of the record.

If you are depending on an outside organization for protection, check its retention practices to ensure that it will maintain your records for as long as you need them.

2. *Planned dispersal.* Another form of protection that makes use of existing copies is planned dispersal. Here an existing copy of the record is sent to an off-site location instead of being disposed of.

3. *Duplicating the record.* For the vast majority of vital records, duplicating the record and storing the copy off-site is the only viable approach. If the records are on a computer-readable medium, a backup copy of the medium is stored off-site. Otherwise, unless the amount of material is extremely small and easily photocopied, microfilming the records is the most practical and cost-effective thing to do.

If the records are on microfilm, the originals should be stored off-site in a climate-controlled location and a working copy of the film kept in the office. Then if a disaster occurs, you can make another first-generation copy from the original. (Films lose quality with each generation, just as photocopies of photocopies are not as clear as photocopies of originals.) In fact, because duplicating microfilm is so inexpensive (the major expense is the filming), it makes sense to make a copy of any film and store the original off-site. I discuss microfilming in detail in Chapter 10.

4. *Protecting the original.* In some very limited circumstances, the original record needs to be protected, such as where a microfilm copy of the original may not be legally acceptable (securities or negotiable instruments, for example) or where the original document is added to daily (a laboratory notebook that is not yet complete). In these cases, store the record in a vault or fire-resistant file cabinet. But if you are going to invest in such equipment, you need to understand both its benefits and its limitations.

First of all, the equipment is expensive. Therefore, you want to use it selectively, not for all vital records. Second, it is heavy. A fire-resistant file cabinet typically weighs over 500 pounds, and, of course, vaults and safes are far heavier. Hence, you'll have to consider whether the floor will tolerate the weight. Finally, you may not be able to access the records quickly after the disaster. A building in which there has been a fire may not be safe to enter for days or even weeks.

On the other hand, properly selected equipment can provide

significant protection. Such equipment is tested by Underwriters Laboratories (UL) and rated for both temperature and time.

The temperature rating means that the cabinet's interior should not go above a certain temperature when the exterior is exposed to intense heat. Equipment with a 350°F limit is designed for paper records. Equipment with a 150°F limit is designed to protect magnetic tape, microfilm, and other photographic records, while 125°F units are required to protect diskettes. A common error is to store microfilm or magnetic media in filing equipment that is only adequate for protecting paper records.

The time limit rating is the length of time the equipment can be exposed to the intense heat without its contents reaching the specified temperature. Most fire-resistant file cabinets are one-hour–rated, while safes and vaults are typically rated for four hours.

A practical tip here: If anyone tells you his records are protected in fire-resistant cabinets, ask to see the equipment. I remember vividly a bank mortgage staff member who assured me that all original signed notes were in "fireproof files." In fact, they were in standard four-drawer file cabinets, which conduct heat beautifully and provide no protection. If you're not sure about a piece of equipment, look for the rating plate, which is usually found inside the top drawer.

The Vital Records Center

By now, you've probably concluded that the majority of your vital records will be protected by storing duplicate copies off-site. The next question is "Where?"

Since most, if not all, of the duplicates will be microfilm or magnetic media, you'll need a climate-controlled facility. While a few very large corporations have found it practical to build their own vital records center, most organizations find it more practical to use a commercial facility.

When selecting a facility, all of the considerations discussed in Chapter 6 for commercial records centers apply. In addition, there is a distance factor. Some companies have a policy that the vital records center be x number of miles away (usually 75 or 150). However, I've always found common sense to be a better guideline. You want the facility far enough away that the same disaster will not destroy both it and your site (75 miles up or down the Atlantic coast in a hurricane zone won't do it). On the other hand, if you're in New York, there's no point using a vital records facility in Utah. So consider, too, how quickly you need access to your records if a disaster occurs.

The Vital Records Schedule

After all the decisions have been made as to what records are to be protected, how this is to be done, and where the records will be kept, this information needs to be documented.

Since only a small percentage of a company's records are vital, this schedule will be much shorter than the retention schedule. Just as with the retention schedule, the easiest approach is to create a database and print out the schedule.

Typical database fields are:

- *Record title.* This should match the title on the retention schedule. It's also a good idea to indicate on the retention schedule if a record is vital.
- *Media* (e.g., paper, microfilm, magnetic tape).
- *Location of copies.*
- *Frequency of deposit.* How much data can you afford to lose? With magnetic media, the backup is usually updated daily. However, with paper records, this is not usually practical. For example, with laboratory notebooks, the decision might be to film them after completion and to store them in a fire-resistant file cabinet until they are completed.
- *Department responsible for making the deposit.* If this isn't the records management department, be sure to have adequate safeguards to ensure that records are copied and deposited off-site on schedule.
- *Retention.* Sometimes a record is not classified as vital for its entire life span; as a result, the retention schedule value may not be appropriate here.

Testing the Vital Records Program

Just as your company holds (or should hold) periodic fire drills, so should it also test the vital records program to ensure that it will function properly if a disaster occurs. The first step in the test is picking the team of employees who would have to reconstruct operations in the event of a disaster. The employees are then given a set of information needs the organization would have after the disaster. Using only the protected records, the employees must demonstrate that they can re-create the data and provide the appropriate information.

Here are some sample test problems:

- Continue to pay employees on time and make all proper payroll deductions.
- Prepare a current inventory of all company assets.
- Send revised shipping instructions to vendors with outstanding orders.
- Prepare an insurance claim for a particular location. (You may want to discuss the matter with the insurance company to determine what kind of documentation it needs to honor the claim.)
- Collect all information needed to resume manufacture of a particular product or to resume service in a certain area.

Most organizations that have a program and test it do so annually. The consensus is that testing is one of the most valuable steps in the process. I've yet to find a company that did not discover "holes" in its program when the test was done. Tests also keep employees alert and prepared to cope with a crisis.

Keeping the Program Up-to-Date

Just as the retention schedule is revised annually, so should the vital records program. Any new record categories created in the past year should be reviewed to determine if they are vital. Doing the revision after the annual test is a good approach because you can correct any flaws that the test revealed.

If a Disaster Does Occur

Hopefully you'll never find out how well the program works. However, disasters do happen, and even if the program has protected all essential records, there will be other records you would like to recover, as well as those that will be totally destroyed.

Your first priority is to salvage recoverable records. Your microfilm or computer systems vendor may be able to recommend one of the professional firms that specialize in saving records damaged by water or other causes. Also most libraries know of firms that specialize in recovering damaged documents. If you have water-damaged film or magnetic media, do *not* try to dry them out on your own. Contact a professional. If you identify qualified professionals now—not after the disaster—you'll know whom to call should the worst happen.

Of course, some records will be unrecoverable. In this situation, document as much as possible what these records were. Then if the company should be asked to produce them for litigation or some other purpose, you'll be able to explain why they are not available. For example, when one California firm's records center was damaged in a mud slide, the records on the lower shelves were not recoverable. To forestall future problems, the records manager took photographs of the damage and used the records center index to prepare a list of the destroyed records.

9

Managing the
Organization's Files

Up to now, we've dealt primarily with inactive records. For many organizations, that's where their records management program stops. Individual departments are allowed to maintain their active working records any way they wish. This system can create substantial problems. Secretaries may develop filing systems they alone understand, so problems arise when they're absent. Several departments may keep unnecessary and costly duplicate files instead of sharing one common set of information. The wrong types of filing equipment may be selected, thus slowing retrieval and wasting both space and money. And finally, when the records go to inactive storage, they may be in an order intelligible only to the original filer—thus complicating retrieval.

All of these problems arise from the fact that many departments do not have the expertise to establish the most effective filing systems and do not regard filing as a priority—at least, not until they are unable to find a record. Hence, it makes sense to involve professionals—the records management staff—in departmental filing systems.

Uniform Filing Systems

One way to reduce departmental filing problems is to establish a uniform filing system. Such a system superimposes a "master" subject filing system on all of the company's records. A uniform filing system is virtually a must when files are centralized in one area because it greatly simplifies retrieval, groups related records together, and eliminates the accidental storage of duplicate records.

Uniform filing systems can also be used effectively when departments maintain their own files. With this approach, each department classifies and maintains its records according to the uniform system, thus saving the time normally spent in designing its own system. And if the company decides later to convert to central files, the process is much simpler if the uniform system is already in use. The uniform system makes it possible to locate quickly any file, regardless of where it is kept. It also eliminates miscellaneous files, as every document has a place within the system, and simplifies training, as employees only have to learn one filing system.

Developing a Uniform System

Unfortunately, you can't buy a standard uniform filing system and simply impose it on your records. Different organizations have different types of records, so the subject categories for classifying these records vary. As a result, you'll need to develop a system unique to your organization.

Developing a uniform filing system does require significant amounts of time and energy. While the benefits are substantial, it's not a task to be undertaken lightly. Also, if the system is implemented in a decentralized program where individual departments maintain their own files, some system of monitoring, such as files audits, is necessary to ensure that departments comply with the program.

As a first step, use the data from the records inventory and the retention schedule to select major subject headings for the system. Or, if you prefer, you can prepare the retention schedule and the uniform filing system simultaneously.

Choose appropriate alpha codes for each heading. Unlike numeric codes, alpha codes instantly remind users of the subjects they represent. Some typical main headings and codes are:

ADM	Administration
ENG	Engineering
FIN	Finance and accounting
HUM	Human resources
LEG	Legal
MFG	Manufacturing
MKT	Marketing

These headings do not refer specifically to the records of various departments; rather, they include *all* corporate records pertaining to a subject. For example, finance department records on its employees fall under the category of human resources, while the human resources budget records belong under finance. Avoid subject headings such as "forms," "correspondence," and "reports," which indicate the format of the information rather than its contents.

Each subject heading and subheading should have a clear written definition, such as "finance and accounting: records pertaining to all financial and accounting activities, including general accounting, tax, payroll, budget, cash management, and investments." Written definitions ensure that records are properly classified.

Limit the number of main headings, as too many headings make it difficult for users to categorize records correctly. As a general rule, the number of main headings should not exceed thirty. I usually find that fifteen or fewer headings are all that are needed.

Next, develop subheadings for each main category. For example, "finance and accounting" might be subdivided as follows:

FIN 01	General accounting
FIN 02	Accounts receivable
FIN 03	Accounts payable
FIN 04	Treasury and cash management

    FIN 05   Payroll
    FIN 06   Taxes
    . . .   . . .

As you develop the system, you will probably note areas that overlap. For example, should payroll taxes be located under FIN 05 or under FIN 06? (Personally, I'd put them under FIN 05, as they are an integral part of the payroll system and administered by that group.)

Each of the subheadings is divided one more time. For example, FIN 03 (accounts payable) might be broken down as follows:

    FIN 03-01   Vendor invoices
    FIN 03-02   Employee expense reports
    FIN 03-03   Accounts payable reports
    . . .   . . .

Note that with the first two items, we have now reached actual records that would then be filed in whatever way is appropriate (invoices by vendor number, for example). The third item, the reports, would then be broken down one more time into the various reports (FIN 03-03-01, FIN 03-03-02, . . .). By the third or fourth breakout, you should have reached actual records categories. A system involving more than three or four levels of classification becomes too complicated, and your records will be categorized incorrectly.

So that the classification process is kept as simple as possible, the uniform filing system should be supported by a detailed alphabetic index that lists each record under all of its possible names. For example, the company's federal income tax return might be indexed under "IRS Form 1120," "federal income tax return," and "income tax return—federal." Be sure to index all reports and forms by their form or report number as well as by their names.

A key to a successful filing system is user input. I usually prepare a draft version based on the inventory data. Then I submit the draft to the users for feedback, make any necessary revisions, and resubmit it. After everyone agrees on the draft, I try to test the system by converting a limited number of records. The test often reveals areas that need to be corrected or situations that had not been foreseen.

Of course, training is needed for all individuals who will be using the system. And to ensure consistency throughout the organization, all changes to the system must be cleared through the records management area.

On a smaller scale, these guidelines can also be applied to developing a subject filing system for an individual department's records. With any subject filing system, the main difficulty is proper classification of documents. Here, the key to success is keeping subject categories simple and clearly defined and using experienced filing staff.

Filing Individual Record Categories

A uniform filing system imposes an overall order on records, but how do you determine the best way to file individual records categories—for example, "employee personnel files," "litigation files," or "sales orders"? No one filing system is appropriate for all categories, so you must choose the best system for each category.

Alphabetic Filing by Name

Filing material alphabetically by name is the oldest, simplest, and most commonly used of all filing systems. Typical applications include personnel files, vendor files, and customer files. The system's primary virtue is its simplicity. No index is needed to find a particular file, and classifying the material to be filed is relatively straightforward.

However, even the simplest system has drawbacks. In an alphabetic system of over 10,000 files, confusion over a name's proper spelling can make retrieval difficult. The name *Burke*, for example, can also be spelled B-e-r-k, B-e-r-k-e, B-i-r-k, B-i-r-k-e, and B-u-r-k. With a small system, finding the correct spelling is relatively easy, but with a large system, searching is time-consuming, costly, and frustrating.

A common error is misfiling ambiguous first and last names. Is it "Scott Leslie" or "Leslie Scott"? An additional problem is errors due to unclear or nonexistent filing rules. For example, is "R. R. Donnelly & Co." filed at the beginning of the Rs, after "Robert's Plumbing," or in the Ds?* One filing system I know of had files for that firm in all three places because different filers made different decisions.

You could solve these problems by developing your own set of standardized filing rules to cover such situations. However, a simple, more effective solution is to adopt ARMA's *Alphabetic Filing Rules* (see References) as the company standard in this area. The rules were recently adopted as an ANSI standard by the American National Standards Institute and can be obtained from ARMA International for a nominal charge.

Numeric Filing Systems

Because of the potential for confusion with a large alphabetic filing system, many organizations assign unique numbers to individual files. Thus, hospitals file your patient record by a patient number, unique to you, thus ensuring that your file is not confused with that of another individual with a similar name. Numeric systems do, of course, require an index to cross-reference the number with what it represents.

There are three basic types of numeric filing systems: consecutive, terminal digit, and middle digit.

1. *Consecutive numeric filing.* Consecutive numeric filing is the simplest of the numeric systems. As the name implies, documents or files are placed in consecutive order according to their assigned number. Such a system works well if you have fewer than 10,000 files. If you have more, several problems arise: It is more time-consuming to file documents with five-digit numbers, and the likelihood of error increases substantially when five, instead of four, digits are filed consecutively.

Also, since the most recently created files are generally the most frequently referenced, filing activity is greatest at the end of

---

* At the beginning of the Rs.

the numeric series. Often several people need to work in the same area and get in each other's way. Finally, when older files at the front end of the series are retired to storage, the remaining files must be moved down to make room for the new files at the end.

2. *Terminal digit filing.* Terminal digit filing was developed to overcome these problems. The terminal digit system is based on the principle of filing "backward" in groups of two or three digits. Each file number is typically divided into three groups. Thus, file 110319 becomes 11 03 19.

The groups are filed in reverse order. All the files ending in 00 come first, then those ending in 01, then those ending in 02, and so on. Next, the files are grouped by their middle digits so that all the 00 01s come before the 01 01s. Finally, the files are arranged by their first digits so that 11 00 01 would precede 12 00 01 which would come before 13 00 01.

Here's an example of how a group of files in terminal digit order would be arranged:

11	01	00
9	02	00
12	03	00
88	02	01
20	10	01
21	10	01
16	09	02

Although this system sounds confusing if you are unfamiliar with it, once filing personnel are trained, fewer misfiles occur. Errors decrease because files personnel are working with groups of two or three digits instead of a long string of five or more. To further enhance its effectiveness, terminal digit filing should be used with color coding (discussed later in this chapter).

With a terminal digit system, the newest—and presumably most heavily referenced—files are spread out throughout the shelves or cabinets instead of concentrated at the end. Consequently, files personnel work uniformly throughout the system, and traffic jams are avoided. Also when older files are pulled for storage or destruction, they are pulled throughout the system, thus eliminating the need to shift files down.

Terminal digit filing is typically used for large, active numeric files such as hospital patient records, insurance policy files, and bank loan files.

3. *Middle digit filing.* One of the advantages of terminal digit filing can also be a disadvantage: If you want to retrieve one hundred consecutively numbered files, you must go to one hundred different locations in the filing system. Middle digit filing was designed to eliminate that problem and is used for the same types of files as terminal digit systems.

Just as the name implies, filing begins with the middle grouping of digits. Then the records are filed by the first group of digits, and finally by the last group. As the example below shows, files whose middle digits are 00 would be first, then 01, and so on.

1	00	22
1	00	23
12	00	01
5	01	20
6	01	19
6	01	20
16	01	01

Because 100 consecutive files, grouped as 1 00 00 to 1 00 99, are located together, it is easier to convert a consecutive numeric system to middle digit filing than to terminal digit. When supplemented by color coding, middle digit, like terminal digit, has a low error rate. One disadvantage is that filing activity is not spread out as evenly as in a terminal digit system. Also, it may take personnel slightly longer to adjust to a middle digit system because the numeric ordering is somewhat more complex.

Computer-Indexing Active Files

If a file needs to be retrieved by more than one identifier, computer indexing becomes desirable. For example, the legal department may want to computer-index contract files by:

- Name of the other party to the contract;
- Department within the company involved in the contract; and
- Date the contract expires or is up for renewal.

Such an index makes it simple to locate all contracts that expired in the past year or all contractual commitments made with a particular company. The actual files can be placed in any order that seems desirable, such as alphabetically by name of the other party or by contract number (an identifying number assigned by the legal department and included in the index).

Any standard PC database package is usually satisfactory for developing such indexes. And, of course, the principles of indexing apply equally to records maintained on nonpaper media such as microfilm or optical disk.

Computer indexing is a valuable tool, but like any such tool it can be misused. Inputting data into the index takes time; hence, the indexing fields should be selected carefully. Indexing files by fields that will not be used is a waste of time and energy. I've seen computer indexing systems where up to thirty minutes were spent indexing each document—in many cases, a wasted effort.

Also, all files do not need computer indexing. If a file needs to be located only by one identifier, simply file it in alphabetic or numeric order. For example, a company with 800 employees will probably find it easiest to keep its personnel files in alphabetic order by last name. On the other hand, it might be beneficial to computer-index job applications and résumés of potential new hires so that they can be searched by the types of position, as well as by applicant name and date of application.

To Centralize or Not?

A separate issue is whether to combine some or all of an organization's active files in one location and what type of overall control to apply to active files.

You have four basic choices:

1. *Central files.* Some or all of the organization's active records are controlled by the records management staff and kept in one or more central file areas. Records are on either hard copy or microfilm.
2. *Electronic central files.* Records are centralized, but users can retrieve and view the records at workstations in their individual work areas.
3. *Controlled decentralized files.* Each department keeps its own files. However, they are maintained in accordance with corporate standards such as a uniform filing system and are audited regularly to ensure compliance.
4. *Decentralized files.* Each department keeps its own active records and retains full control over them.

As you might suspect, the last option, total decentralization, is the least desirable. While some departments will do an excellent job of maintaining their records, others will be less motivated. I can think of at least three large corporate engineering departments where the filing system was random—that is, the engineers put the files in their cabinets as the spirit moved them, not even in date sequence or alphabetically—a problem not unique to engineers. If anyone other than the individual keeping the file needed a record, retrieval was virtually hopeless.

Therefore, any controls you can implement for active records will benefit the organization. Let's consider central files first.

Central Files

With a central files program, all active files except those being created or in current use are kept in one or more central file rooms. These rooms function as libraries, with records being checked out to users and follow-ups conducted if the records are not returned on time.

Central files provide the following advantages:

• Fewer misfiles and lost records because all filing is done by professionals whose sole job is to operate the file room
• More efficient use of office space through the elimination of duplicate records and the use of space-efficient high-

density filing equipment (to be discussed later in this chapter)
- More effective use of clerical staff through the elimination of time spent filing duplicates
- Improved compliance with the retention schedule because the central files staff ensures that records are sent to storage or disposed of on schedule
- A thorough knowledge, and consequently a more effective use, of the information kept within the organization

With such a formidable list of benefits, you may wonder why every organization doesn't adopt a central files system. There are two main difficulties. The first difficulty is that sometimes, it's just physically impractical; the way a building is constructed may mean that there is no space for a central file area. Also if a company's facilities are spread over a wide area, centralizing active records in one location is impractical and inefficient. Such a company might consider a number of central file areas, each serving the users at a particular site.

The second difficulty is that users often resist the idea. Most users want *their* records at *their* fingertips. Therefore, establishing a central files system usually must be mandated by senior management. However, I don't want to give you the impression that centralizing files means creating a records dictatorship. Having installed a number of central file rooms, I can assure you that while there is initial resistance, before the first year's anniversary, most users will extoll the virtues of central filing and will wonder how they ever got along without it.

These simple guidelines will help you defuse user resistance and make the program a success.

1. *Make sure the central file area is conveniently located for users.* If people have to walk half a mile or go down five floors to retrieve their records, they will be reluctant to send their files to a central location.

2. *Don't introduce a central files concept until you already have a successful records management program in other areas.* For example, if users have confidence in the records center for

storing inactive records, they are more likely to trust their active records to central files.

3. *Enlist strong senior management support.* Corporate policy should require user compliance with the program. In addition to policy, visible support from top management helps. When the CEO at one company asked that his files be inventoried and incorporated into the central files system, other managers were quick to follow his example.

4. *Establish the program gradually.* Bring one department's records into the file area at a time. Otherwise, you'll have confusion and frustrated users. It's also a good idea to start with departments or groups who are less violently opposed to the program. Leave the highly resistant groups to last. They'll soon see that the program is working smoothly, and it will be harder for them to oppose it.

5. *Communicate with the users.* Get user input on procedures, such as for submitting and retrieving records. Once the room is operational, invite everyone to an open house, as suggested in Chapter 2. Some homemade cookies or other "goodies" will encourage people to come, and seeing a well-organized facility does much to reduce resistance.

6. *Do not allow users to retrieve or refile records.* Central files personnel must handle these duties if the integrity of the files is to be preserved and misfiles kept to a minimum.

7. *Either follow up on checked-out records or don't check them out.* If you don't follow up on checked-out documents, you may go to retrieve a record and find out it was checked out a year ago, the person that had it left six months ago, and no one knows here it is.

Your other alternative is to prohibit people from taking originals from the room. In this case, small work areas must be made available to users for referencing documents. When a user needs to take a record out, a photocopy is made. While this may seem cumbersome, if the documents are essential to the organization, it's a wise precaution. Many pharmaceutical companies follow this practice with documents that must be available for regulatory agency review. If you do opt for the photocopying approach, be sure to identify clearly that the copies are duplicates and should not be filed. Either stamp the copy as such or print it on paper that has the word *copy* screened on it.

8. *Make sure file room hours are adequate for user needs.* Organizations on "flextime" often stagger file room staffing and lunch hours so that the room is open for a wide range of hours, such as 7:30 A.M. to 6:00 P.M. And if a record might be needed after hours in an emergency, have a procedure for reaching records staff at home to retrieve the records. (Don't be unduly nervous about this. I've found that emergency retrievals are virtually nonexistent, but users feel greatly comforted by the fact that an emergency procedure exists.)

9. *Consider carefully whether highly confidential records should be kept in the central files.* Many organizations exclude legal, payroll, and personnel records from central files, preferring to have mini-central files in those areas.

10. *Consider using central files selectively.* The selective approach means that files referenced by several departments (a bank's mortgage files) or essential to the organization's existence (a pharmaceutical company's clinical study files and FDA submissions) are kept in central files. And records primarily of interest to one department are maintained in that department.

Electronic Central Files

The option of storing records on optical disks (or, in some cases, microfilm) completely eliminates the need for users to go to the file room. When a record is needed, they call it up on their workstations and either view the document there or print a hard copy on a laser printer.

I discuss such systems in considerably more detail in Chapters 10 and 11. While these systems offer many advantages, they are a relatively new and costly technology.

Controlled Decentralized Files—The Compromise

For many companies, a controlled decentralized system represents the ideal compromise between central files and decentralization. For others, the system serves as a stepping-stone on the way to central filing.

With a controlled decentralized system, each department keeps and maintains its own active records. But the records management staff reviews the department's filing system to ensure consistency throughout the organization—for example, requiring all departments to use standard alphabetic filing rules such as those prepared by ARMA International. If a uniform filing system exists, the department follows it. The records management staff also assists the department in establishing internal filing procedures.

While a controlled decentralized system does not eliminate duplicate records, it helps ensure that departments maintain files in accordance with overall organizational guidelines. For such an approach to be effective, departmental compliance with these guidelines should be monitored through annual files audits.

The Files Audit

Although the records management department can conduct files audits, it's usually preferable for you to have the internal audit department perform them as part of its standard operational auditing procedure. This practice has several advantages, the most important being that the internal audit team has clout; department heads know that they must comply with its findings. Also, you incur less user resentment if your group does not actually perform the audit. Finally, the records management team has enough to do without conducting audits. If, however, there is no internal audit department, the responsibility is yours.

No matter who conducts the audit, as records manager, it's your responsibility to set the standards. Typically, these include:

- Legible, accurate labels on all file drawers, shelves, and folders
- No overcrowding (drawers and shelves should have at least 3 inches of free space)
- Use of OUT cards (if you don't see any, there's a problem)
- Use of a follow-up system to ensure that checked-out records are returned

- Conformity with the uniform filing system, if one exists
- Existence of an up-to-date index where appropriate
- Compliance with the retention schedule

The auditors should also interview both files personnel and users to find out if any problems exist or if either group has any suggestions for improving the system.

A files audit is not a trap to get people in trouble; it's a device to maintain quality. Departments should know the audit standards well in advance of the audit, although they need not know when the audit will occur.

As a backup to the audits (or in place of them, if audits are impractical at this time), implement an organizational policy that all purchases of filing equipment must be approved by the records management staff. Whenever a department requests filing equipment, conduct a quick audit to make sure the department is in compliance with the retention schedule and has a legitimate need for the equipment. This is a remarkably effective tool for identifying organizational "pack rats." It also ensures that departments purchase filing equipment that is best suited to their needs.

Filing Equipment

Before you can select the right filing equipment for a particular situation, you must consider the following factors:

- *Access frequency and retrieval speed.* Drawer filing systems are slower than shelf systems. If records are accessed heavily, fast retrieval is a key factor. Also, with some types of equipment, all of the records are not physically available at the same time. This may be a problem if extremely rapid retrieval is needed.

- *Filing features.* What size and type are the records—legal-size, letter-size, computer printouts, three-ring binders? Does the entire file folder need to be pulled or just selected items from it?

You should find your need for legal-size file cabinets diminishing. ARMA International's Project ELF (Eliminate Legal Files) has been quite successful in convincing courts to require materials on letter-size paper. Most of the legal-size cabinets I see are filled with letter-size materials. Since legal-size cabinets and filing supplies cost more and consume more space, be sure you use them only when necessary.

• *Space requirements.* Must the equipment fit in a particular area?

• *Space cost vs. equipment cost.* If you're in a high-rent district, more expensive equipment that can hold a large number of records in a small space may be cost-justified.

• *Building structure.* Some of the more space-efficient filing equipment requires reinforced floors.

• *Security.* How confidential are the records? Filing equipment locks provide limited security. Often a number of cabinets can be opened with the same key, and obtaining duplicate keys is usually easy to do. Also such locks can be "popped open" fairly easily. Files that need to be really secure should be kept in a room that is always locked when unattended.

• *Fire protection.* As discussed in Chapter 8, standard filing cabinets do not provide fire protection. Records deemed vital need some form of extra protection.

• *Mobility.* Some types of filing equipment are built-in and costly to move.

• *System growth.* The system should be able to meet future needs as well as present criteria.

Keeping these considerations in mind, let's look at the various types of filing equipment.

Vertical File Cabinets

The vertical file cabinet is the oldest of the filing equipment options. Although lately it's been maligned, primarily because it's been misused, the vertical file is still a good choice for storing records in individual offices or small departments. However, if more than four vertical file cabinets are needed in an area, you should consider other options; at that point the cabinets no longer use space efficiently.

Vertical files do require 44 inches of aisle space for pulling out drawers. Five-drawer cabinets provide more filing capacity than four-drawer cabinets for the same amount of floor space. However, unless your filing team is composed of professional basketball players, you may find that your staff has difficulty seeing into the top drawer.

Since drawers must be opened, retrieval and filing are relatively slow. Also, only one person can use a file cabinet at a time. However, a retrieval/filing advantage is that a user can add or remove documents from a folder without taking the entire folder from the cabinet.

Lateral Filing Cabinets

Lateral cabinets (see photograph) have gained great popularity in recent years, partly because they are more attractive than vertical cabinets and partly because they fit in areas where vertical files

Lateral filing equipment.

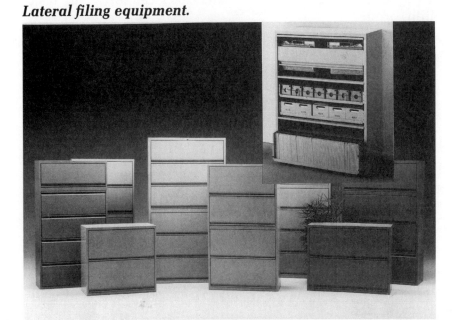

Courtesy Tab Products Company.

may not, since they require only 30 inches of aisle space. Laterals do, of course, require more wall space.

Records may be filed either sideways or from front to back as in a vertical file. Like vertical files, lateral cabinets are best suited for individual offices and small departmental records collections.

Since laterals are a drawer system, the same access and retrieval speed qualifications apply as to vertical cabinets. Also, five-drawer cabinets pose the same retrieval problems for shorter people.

Open-Shelf Filing

Shelf filing systems (see photograph) provide faster retrieval than drawer systems and permit simultaneous multiple-user access. Because users do not have to look down into the drawers, the systems can be higher than drawer units, thus adding filing capacity. Additional space is conserved, since there are no drawers to be pulled out. Shelf filing is particularly effective when used with color coding, as a quick visual check can reveal any major filing errors.

The disadvantages are that units must be emptied to be moved and may need to be disassembled. Also, unless the files are in a secure area, there is no deterrent to an unauthorized person's taking a file. In case of fire, the records are susceptible to water damage, as well as harm from the flames.

Compactible files (also called movable or high-density files—see photograph), a variation of open-shelf filing, conserve additional space. The open-shelf files are mounted on tracks imbedded in the floor. The filing units slide along the tracks so users can get to the records they need. Consequently, all records are not available at the same time.

Compactible files do require building alterations (i.e., installing the tracks). Therefore, moving the units to another location is expensive and usually requires vendor assistance. Also, because the file units themselves are heavy and consolidate a great many records in a very small space, you may have to reinforce the floor.

Compactible systems come in three basic types. The first is

Open-shelf filing equipment.

Courtesy Tab Products Company.

totally manual; the user grasps a handle and slides the files along a track. Mechanical-assist systems use a chain and sprocket mechanism, similar to that in a bicycle, to make moving the files easier. Then there are totally automated versions; here, all the user has to do is press a button and the files open at the desired point.

The length of the shelving rows, the height of the units, the weight of the materials to be stored on the shelves, and the number of rows of shelves determine which type of system is most appropriate.

Compactible files are an extremely space-efficient equipment option for central file rooms. Also, the units can (and should) be closed up at night and locked to protect the records from water damage in case of a fire. Also the records are better protected from fire damage if the unit is closed.

Compactible files.

Courtesy Tab Products Company.

Motorized Files

Motorized files bring the record to the user. Files are stored on shelves in a large, enclosed metal unit that looks like a huge box. The operator sits before the unit and presses a button to indicate the appropriate shelf, which is then automatically moved into position in front of the operator for retrieval.

Motorized files do provide fast access with a minimum of operator effort, and the units do store large numbers of records in a small amount of space. However, only one person can use a unit at a time.

Moreover, the units are extremely expensive in terms of cost, installation, and maintenance. If you decide on this option, you will need a service contract, and if your company is not located in a major metropolitan area, timely repairs can be a problem. While the files can usually be hand-cranked if there is a breakdown, this process is very slow and cumbersome.

Since motorized files are extremely heavy, you will have to

consider reinforcing the floor. Additional drawbacks are that the files must be installed by a vendor, moving the units is quite costly, and partially filled units must be loaded in such a way that filing weight is evenly distributed throughout the unit.

As you've probably guessed, I don't advocate these units for most filing situations (but I think that smaller motorized units specifically designed for storing card files, microfilm, microfiche, and aperture cards can be useful). Money could be better spent converting your paper records to another medium. Generally, I feel that motorized files are an expensive short-term solution only.

Color Coding Your Files

A relatively inexpensive adjunct to your filing systems and equipment, color coding speeds the retrieval and refiling of records while reducing misfiles. As an added benefit, it brightens the entire office environment when used with an open-shelf filing system.

For numeric filing systems, a different color is used for each digit from 0 to 9, creating bands of colors in the files and making it easy to spot a misplaced folder. Thus, in a terminal digit system, if 1 is red and 7 blue, all files with numbers ending in 17 form a red and blue band. But usually you don't want to color code all digits in a number; too heavy a use of color creates visual confusion.

For alphabetic systems, a different color is assigned to each letter—usually only the first two letters of the last name are coded this way. Color-coded year labels ensure that a 1991 file doesn't accidentally get placed in the 1990 section.

A wide range of color-coded systems are available. While most systems are designed for the side-tab file folders used in shelf filing, some color coding supplies are available for top-tab folders used in file drawers.

Another possibility is using colored folders to differentiate files that might otherwise be confused. However, they cost more than their manila counterparts, so be sure you have a good reason for using them.

However you elect to use color in your files, keep the sys-

tem(s) simple and easy to remember. Use distinctive colors that
stand out clearly. And remember, color does not eliminate the
need for a logical filing system, but it does support and enhance
the system.

Out Cards

Not only do OUT cards identify who has a record, they also speed
refiling, as the files person can go directly to the card.

OUT cards come in two basic varieties. The first is the card
stock version where you write who took what file directly on the
card. The second (and the one I prefer) is vinyl and comes with
two pockets. The smaller pocket holds a charge-out slip, and the
larger one holds any documents that may have come in for the
file while it was checked out.

Your major difficulty with OUT cards will be in getting
people to use them—no problem in a central file room where filing personnel realize that the cards make their lives easier. But if
users are accessing the files directly, they're almost always in
"too much of a hurry" to complete a card. I've had some success
with assigning a different color card to each individual. This approach seems to appeal to the user's ego: "These are *my* cards,
and no one else can use them."

Bar Coding

If you allow users to check files out from the central file room,
consider implementing an automated checkout and retrieval system. The principle is virtually identical to that used in library
charge-out systems. The folders are all bar-coded. When a user
checks out a file, the file bar code and the user's bar code are
scanned into the system. When the file is returned, it's rescanned.
Such systems provide a fast, easy way to monitor file activity.
Most commercial records management software packages have
bar-coding modules available.

The Floating File

At one time or another, virtually every file room faces the problem of the "floating file": The person who checked out the file passes it on to someone else without notifying the file room. The second individual passes it on to a third, and so on. When the records staff tries to locate the file, the person who originally checked it out responds, "I gave it to so-and-so a week and a half ago." The records staff must then track the elusive file.

The only way to avoid the problem completely is not to check out files. However, that may be impractical, in which case one of the following three actions will help:

1. Establish a policy that the person checking out the file is responsible for it until he or she either returns it or notifies you that it has been passed on.
2. Shorten the time period for following up on checked-out records. That way, files don't travel as far.
3. Attach routing forms to each file. Then if the file is transferred, the person transferring it simply removes a routing form, writes down who took the file, and sends it to central files.

Paper—Here to Stay

While document imaging is an increasingly large part of the records management scene (as we'll see in the following chapters), the records manager is making a grave mistake if he or she ignores paper files. While paper is not glamorous or "sexy," it is still the predominant records medium and will continue to be so for some time to come. Your key to success is identifying the best medium for each record category and then designing an effective system using that medium.

10

Document Imaging
Micrographics

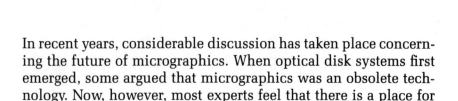

In recent years, considerable discussion has taken place concerning the future of micrographics. When optical disk systems first emerged, some argued that micrographics was an obsolete technology. Now, however, most experts feel that there is a place for both technologies and that both will coexist in the marketplace for many years.

The truth is that each technology has its strengths and weaknesses. As records manager, you must evaluate the various applications within the company and identify the most appropriate media. For some organizations, this means using both imaging technologies, while for others, one type of system meets their needs. In this chapter and in Chapter 11, I examine both types of systems and provide you with guidelines for making the right choices.

Microfilm

Let's begin by defining a few terms. *Microfilm* is a fine-grain high-resolution film that can record images greatly reduced in size.

Microfilm may be either roll film or microfiche. *Microform* is another name for the various film formats. *Micrographics* refers to the science or art of recording images on microfilm.

Advantages

When we think of the advantages of microfilm, space savings immediately spring to mind. Microfilmed records typically save up to 95 percent of the space occupied when records are kept on paper. These space savings are also reflected in a reduction in filing equipment.

A bigger advantage is improved access to records. Usually documents on film can be referenced more quickly than their hard-copy counterparts: A seated customer service representative can retrieve and reference a microfilm file without leaving his or her desk or even putting down the phone. Also, because film can be duplicated easily and relatively inexpensively, individuals who need their own copies of records can have them. And if a paper copy is needed—to send to a customer, for example—it can be made quickly and easily.

Records protection is another advantage. As discussed in Chapter 8, duplicate sets of film can be stored off-site for a minimal cost. File integrity is preserved because documents are filmed in a fixed, unalterable sequence. And, if certain conditions are met, microfilm is generally admissible as evidence in a court of law. Microfilm is also our most durable media. Archival microfilm will last for hundreds of years.

Limitations

Although microfilm has many advantages, there are also some definite limitations that must be considered when you're deciding whether or not to film records. The most obvious consideration is the need for a piece of equipment—a reader—to view the film. Since a microfilm reader does not replace a computer terminal, the user may need two pieces of equipment in his or her work area.

There are also limitations as to what can be filmed, depending on the type of camera used (different types handle different kinds of documents). The physical condition of the document has a direct impact on film quality.

Unless you're using an updatable microfiche system, there is a time lag between when documents are filmed and when the film is ready for use. Likewise, updating files can be a problem unless you're using updatable microfiche, jackets, or computer-assisted retrieval.

Last, but not least, the issue of user resistance to film must be considered. Many people consider microfilm difficult to use or feel that they can't obtain good hard copies. In reality, today's reader-printers produce excellent plain paper copies. And if documents are properly filmed and indexed, the film will be easy to reference and use. Demonstrating these facts to potential users is usually the easiest way to overcome resistance.

Microforms

Before I discuss performing a micrographics needs analysis, let's consider the various forms microfilm can take and the equipment options.

Serialized Microforms

Serialized microforms (the various types of roll film) are so named because documents are accessed sequentially; that is, you advance through the roll of film until you reach the image you want. The major difficulty with roll film is locating the image you want. Computer indexing of film has done much to reduce this difficulty.

Since duplicating rolls of film is more costly than duplicating individual microfiche, roll film is most effective when a film collection can be shared by a group of users or is kept in a library-type reference center.

The two primary types of serialized microfilm are open-reel film and cartridges. Just as the name implies, open-reel film is an open spool of microfilm. Open-reel film is the least expensive microform and is commonly used in 16mm or 35mm widths. Roll film that is 105mm wide is usually cut into microfiche. Normally, 16mm film is used for correspondence, checks, and letter- and legal-size documents; 35mm film is used for engineering drawings, newspapers, and other oversize materials.

Open-reel film is less protected than cartridges. It is generally used for backup copies or when the film is cut into strips for one of the unitized formats.

Cartridges are a refinement of the open-reel concept. Here the roll of film is encased in plastic to protect it. Cartridges are easy to use and are the most common microform for use in computer-assisted retrieval (CAR) film systems. As might be expected, cartridges are more expensive than open-reel film.

Unitized Microforms

Unlike their serialized counterparts, unitized microforms permit direct access to data without the user's having to advance through a roll of film. Unitized microforms are inexpensive to duplicate and require less expensive readers than roll film.

Consequently, unitized microforms are well-suited for situations where a large number of users need film copies of records. The main unitized categories—aperture cards, card jackets, jackets, and microfiche—are shown in Exhibit 10-1.

Aperture cards are primarily used for engineering drawings. Each eighty-column keypunch card contains one drawing on one frame of 35mm film. You're probably saying, "But no one uses keypunch cards anymore." Well, this is a case of the "well-trodden path." While it is true that keypunch cards are obsolete, companies have been filming engineering drawings on aperture cards for many years. All of the equipment—e.g., readers, reader-printers, filing cabinets—has been designed to accommodate the keypunch card size. Since companies have significant financial investments in this equipment, movements to shift to another size of card have not been successful.

Card jackets are index cards with sleeves for inserting strips of 16mm film. As with the aperture card, eyeball-readable information is combined with filmed images. Card jackets are useful when twenty or fewer pages per file need to be filmed, and having some immediately visible data is helpful. For example, a school might microfilm transcripts and insert them in card jackets. The

Exhibit 10-1.   Unitized microforms.

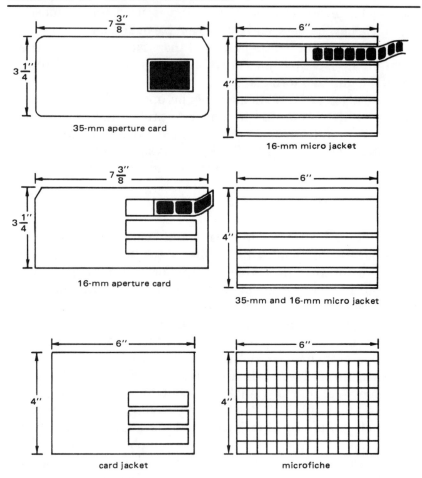

35-mm aperture card

16-mm micro jacket

16-mm aperture card

35-mm and 16-mm micro jacket

card jacket

microfiche

student's name and number and the dates transcripts were sent out would be immediately visible on the card.

Jackets are transparent acetate or polyester carriers with sleeves for inserting film. The jacket, in effect, allows you to convert roll film to a format similar to microfiche. Jackets are updated by adding additional strips of film as needed until the jacket is full. The film is inserted mechanically by a device known as a jacket loader. While jackets holding five strips of 16mm film are most common, jackets holding both 16mm and

35mm film are also available. These jackets can be used to combine engineering drawings and supporting data in one easily duplicatable package.

While jackets do permit continual updating, it is labor-intensive to load the jackets. If there are a number of one- and two-page updates for files, using jackets can become very time-consuming.

Our final unitized microform is the most commonly used—microfiche. A microfiche is a sheet of film containing a number of images or frames in a grid pattern. The reduction level determines the number of frames. For example, if documents are filmed at 24X (reduced to ¼₄ of their original size), the equivalent of ninety-eight 8 ½- by 11-inch pages can be held on fiche. If the reduction level is 42X (¼₂ of original size), 208 frames will fit on one fiche. And at 48X, the fiche will hold 270 frames. A 24X reduction is common for source document (hard-copy) microfilming; 42X and 48X are used for computer-generated microfiche. By comparison, a 100-foot roll of 16mm microfilm typically contains 2,500 to 3,000 letter-size pages.

Traditional source document microfiche are not updatable, but updatable microfiche systems are available. With such fiche, additional documents can be filmed on the master copy as desired, thus making the microfiche the equivalent of a growing paper file. Updatable microfiche are useful for personnel files, customer records, and other files that are added to regularly.

Cameras

The microform(s) you decide to use will determine the type of camera you need; no one camera can produce all of the microforms just described. Cameras fall into two main categories: rotary and planetary.

Rotary Cameras

Rotary cameras (see photograph) are so named because the document and the film move simultaneously during the filming process. Documents are fed into the camera either manually or

Rotary camera with automatic bar code indexing.

Courtesy 3M.

automatically. Then both the documents and the film advance together, and the documents emerge from the camera.

Most rotary cameras use 16mm cartridge or open-reel film. Some models can film both sides of a document simultaneously—called duplex filming. Others—"simplex" filming—film only one side.

Rotary cameras are noted for their speed. The amount of documents filmed in an hour will depend on the documents' size and physical condition and the camera's capabilities. However, with automatic document feed, it's possible to film 1,700 or more documents per hour.

While rotaries are the fastest type of camera, they are also the most limiting. Not only must the material being filmed be single sheets, but very thin or very thick materials may present problems. Also, because materials pass through the camera, rotary filming requires careful document preparation; tears must be taped, very small documents have to be affixed to larger sheets, and so on.

Planetary Cameras

Planetary cameras (see photograph) are so named because both the document and the film remain stationary during the filming process. The material to be filmed is placed on a copy board with exterior lighting mounted on both sides. The filming unit (the actual camera portion of the equipment) is mounted above the copy board and can be raised or lowered to change the reduction level. The resulting image is of a higher quality than that produced by a rotary camera because both the document and film remain stationary.

Planetary cameras come in a variety of sizes. The larger models are used for filming engineering drawings and other oversize documents on 35mm film. Smaller cameras are used for filming letter- and legal-size materials on 16mm film. Traditionally, filming with a planetary camera has been much slower than with a rotary camera because an operator must handle each document. However, planetary cameras with automatic document feeds are now coming close to the speed of rotaries while retaining high image quality.

Planetary camera with automatic document feed.

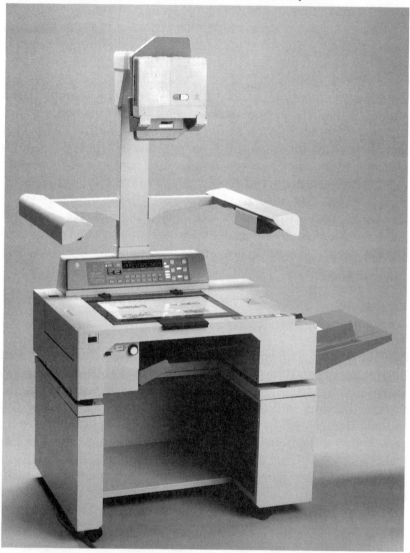

Courtesy Minolta Corporation.

A variation of the planetary camera is the step-and-repeat camera. These cameras prepare microfiche by exposing a series of separate images on the film according to a previously established format or grid. The camera "steps" the film into position for the next exposure and then "repeats" the filming process. Since the microfiche produced are not updatable, step-and-repeat cameras are used mainly in the micropublishing industry.

Camera Processors

Camera processors film the material and then develop the film. They fall into two major categories. First are the special units used to prepare updatable microfiche. It usually takes approximately eight seconds to add an image to an updatable microfiche. Second are units that prepare strips of 16mm film. The strips emerge processed and can then be loaded into jackets.

Film

There are also more than one type of film. Silver gelatin microfilm (also called wet silver because liquid chemicals are used to process it) is primarily used for original rolls, although it can also be used for duplicates. This is the only type of film that meets the archival standards set by ANSI (American National Standards Institute). To qualify as archival, the film must be processed and stored in accordance with the appropriate ANSI standards. Archival film is considered permanent (i.e., good for hundreds of years). Of course, many filming applications do not require archival quality.

Dry silver film is processed by heat instead of chemicals. While it is not archival, if stored under appropriate conditions, it is considered long-term (i.e., will last for 100 years). Dry silver film is frequently used for COM (computer output microfilm), which I discuss later in this chapter.

Diazo and vesicular film are used for duplicate microfilm copies. Ammonia is used to develop diazo film, while a heat process is used for vesicular film. Users generally prefer the quality of diazo copies, but if the copies are made in-house, either a self-venting duplicator is needed or else the ammonia fumes must be vented. Both diazo and vesicular film are considered long-term if properly stored.

The updatable microfiche systems use special types of film, which vary with the vendor. These films, too, are considered long-term if properly stored.

Unless you are using updatable microfiche, the original film should be stored off-site in a climate-controlled facility. Users should work with a duplicate copy. Storing the original off-site ensures that you have backup protection if the copy is accidently injured or destroyed. It's preferable to store the original off-site instead of a copy, as some quality is lost with each generation of film—just as a photocopy of a photocopy will not be as sharp as a photocopy of the original. By protecting the original, you'll always be able to work off a first-generation copy.

While the ANSI standards for film storage vary with the type of film, the two basic issues are temperature and humidity. For long-term or archival storage, the maximum temperature should not exceed 21°C (70°F). Although different types of film can tolerate different levels of relative humidity, the 30 to 40 percent range is satisfactory for all types.

It is important to periodically check any film stored off-site in accordance with the appropriate ANSI standard. This way you can make sure that no deterioration has occurred (see the References for a listing of major micrographics standards).

Readers

Readers and reader-printers are, of course, an essential part of any micrographics system. Consider whether the unit(s) will be compatible with the microforms you plan to use. In addition to equipment specifically designed for microfiche or for roll film, there are universal units that can be adapted for different microforms.

In selecting a reader, determine how heavily it will be used. If it will be used for extended periods of time, be sure to invest in a top-quality unit. For heavy use, "blowback" of 100 percent or more is desirable. In other words, the image appears as large as or larger than the original document. However, for infrequent viewing of originals with fairly large type, a blowback of 75 percent may be adequate.

Other features that are important if the unit is to be used heavily are adjustable screen angles, matte- or dull-finish screens, and tinted screens.

You will want to take into account the sharpness of the screen image, the illumination, and the focus. The screen image should be uniformly sharp and readable over the entire screen area. The illumination should be comfortable for sustained reading without being either too bright or too dim, and it should be fairly even over the entire screen. Make sure the reader is easy to focus; you shouldn't need to refocus frequently when moving from image to image.

The reader should also be sturdily constructed with a heavy, large base to ensure that it won't be tipped over easily. Maintenance, such as changing bulbs, should be easy to do. And if the unit is a portable, it should be able to withstand drops, bumps, or other "hard knocks."

One last tip: Ask the vendor to bring in samples of different models so that users can try them out to see which one they prefer.

Reader-Printers

In addition to projecting an image on a screen, reader-printers (see photographs) also make hard copies of the image. Reader-printers have improved dramatically in recent years. Now it is possible to get, at a reasonable price, models that make excellent copies on plain paper.

Since you are really buying a photocopier as well as a viewer, it's important to determine how many copies you'll be making. As with photocopiers, different models are geared to handle different levels of copying.

My basic rule is: Be generous with readers; be stingy with reader-printers. Not only do reader-printers cost more than readers, but if they are too available, users may make unnecessary copies instead of just referencing the film.

A microfiche reader-printer.

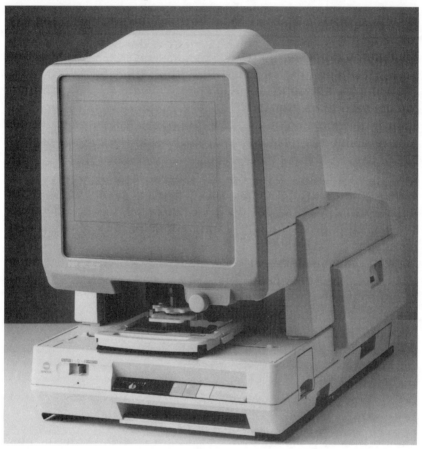

Courtesy Minolta Corporation.

Computer Output Microfilm

Up to now, we've primarily been discussing source document microfilming—converting hard copy to film. However, microfilm can also be generated by computers, thus replacing bulky printouts. Computer output microfilm (COM) is created by a COM recorder (see photograph). If the system is on-line, the recorder receives data directly from the computer and functions as an output device. If the system is off-line, a magnetic tape is mounted

Cartridge microfilm reader-printer.

Courtesy 3M.

A COM recorder.

Courtesy Eastman Kodak Company.

on the recorder's tape drive. In either case, the recorder, in effect, replaces the computer's printer and prints the material directly on microfilm. Some units use dry silver film with a processor built directly into the COM unit.

Depending on the equipment, COM recorders can produce 16mm, 35mm, or 105mm film (microfiche). Most COM is prepared on microfiche using reduction ratios of 42X or 48X. The master microfiche generated by the recorder is then duplicated for distribution to the user.

Some COM recorders function exclusively as alphanumeric printers. Others are also capable of plotting lines and graphics. Another option is the use of forms overlays during the recording process so that the data appear on the form just as they would if they were printed on a hard copy of the form.

Advantages of COM

COM documents have several advantages over their hard-copy counterparts. These include:

1. *Economy.* Film is cheaper than paper. (Remember, we're comparing over 200 pages of printout to one fiche.)
2. *Space savings.* COM reports use 1 to 2 percent of the space occupied by their paper counterparts. Of course, if the report is a daily "throwaway," the space savings may not be a significant advantage.
3. *Faster retrieval.* COM makes it practical for users to keep large reports at their fingertips instead of in a bookcase or off-site in a records center. And the reports can be duplicated inexpensively for everyone who needs them. (A duplicate microfiche costs 10 cents or less.)
4. *Printing speed.* COM recorders print faster than many paper printers.
5. *Postage savings.* Four microfiche, which will hold over 1,000 pages, weigh less than one ounce.
6. *Faster preparation.* COM reports do not need to be decollated, burst, or bound.
7. *Copy quality.* COM reports are of high quality and easy to read.

Limitations of COM

Of course, COM is not the answer to every information need. Data that must be continually updated, such as inventory or reservations systems, are better suited to on-line applications. You may also want to consider COLD (computer output laser disk)—storing the reports on optical disks—an option I discuss in Chapter 11. And, of course, COM has all the limitations of microfilm discussed earlier, such as the need for readers.

User resistance can be a factor as well. With COM, computer reports become little pieces of plastic that can only be read through a machine. The fact that there are no large sheets of paper that can be written on and sent to people frustrates some users.

When faced with such resistance, I find the best approach is to emphasize retrieval speed and cost savings. Some companies encourage conversion to COM by charging users back for hardcopy reports and not charging back for fiche versions. It also helps if prospective users can talk to current users of COM reports.

Other Considerations

Even though the day-to-day responsibility for COM usually falls within the data processing or systems area, it is the records manager's function to promote and encourage the use of COM. In my experience, most organizations do not utilize COM as fully as they could. Many systems departments provide reports on COM only if users request them. Since few users know that they can receive reports on COM or are aware of its benefits, they don't request the service. Consequently, offices and records centers continue to fill up with printouts.

To enhance user satisfaction with COM, solicit input as to how the report should be formatted on the fiche, how each fiche should be titled for easy retrieval, and the most effective way to index the report (the lower right-hand frame contains the index).

If users receive a number of short reports, consider grouping several reports together on one fiche. One caution, though: Don't forget record retention. One organization I know had grouped

A CAR system.

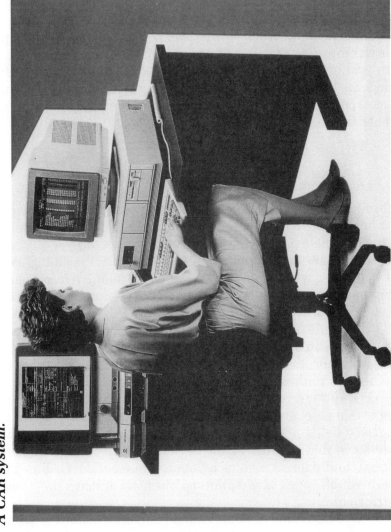

twenty different reports together on a single set of fiche. Most of the reports had a two-year retention, but four had a ten-year retention. Needless to say, those four reports were scattered throughout the set of fiche. It will simplify records disposition considerably if all of the reports in a set of fiche have the same retention period.

Since COM recorders are quite expensive ($100,000 and up), many companies find it more economical to have a service bureau produce COM from their tapes. Service bureau charges are based on volume, and there is usually a minimum monthly charge. Most service bureaus can provide overnight service or a twenty-four-hour turnaround.

Computer-Assisted Retrieval

Not only do computers serve as a source of microfilm, they can also help retrieve information from microfilm. Hence, we have a second acronym: CAR (computer-assisted retrieval).

A CAR system (see photograph) combines the strengths of the computer with the advantages of microfilm. While a computer has the ability to classify and retrieve information quickly in a variety of ways, computer storage has always been expensive—in contrast to microfilm, which can store large amounts of data cheaply in a minimum of space. CAR merges the two technologies. Thus, the computer is used to index data and search for it, while microfilm is used to store and display the information.

CAR systems take a variety of forms. However, the basic concept is that a document is both filmed and computer-indexed by whatever fields are relevant for retrieval. For example, an accounts payable invoice might be indexed by vendor number, amount, and date, as well as by microfilm location. CAR can be used with all types of microforms, but most systems use 16mm cartridge film.

Usually each film frame is encoded below the image with a "blip"—a rectangular mark that identifies the proper frame for retrieval. Three-level blipping is not uncommon: a large blip for each batch of records, a medium-size blip to identify an individual file, and a small blip for each page in the file. Each film frame is also often assigned a unique identifying number.

To retrieve a document, you search the computer database to determine where in the film collection the document is located. Then you retrieve the appropriate film cartridge and insert it in the reader-printer (or reader). Usually the reader-printer is electronically linked to the system so that the film is automatically advanced to the appropriate frame (the reader-printer counts the blips). You can then either view the document on the reader screen or print a hard copy if necessary.

Since documents are located through the computer index, they do not have to be filmed in a particular sequence or order. The labor saved by not having to sort or file the material usually provides one of the major cost justifications for a CAR system.

CAR systems do not offer all of the capabilities of optical disk systems, but they are generally considerably less expensive (however, for single-user, stand-alone systems, optical disk is cheaper). Also the legal acceptability (see Chapter 11) of microfilm is well-established, so hard copy can normally be destroyed after the film is checked.

On the other hand, because it is costly to make a number of sets of roll film, CAR is usually best-suited to departmental applications or when the film collection is managed in a central file area. In the latter instance, the records staff retrieves the film and makes hard copies of the appropriate documents for users.

If you're considering implementing a CAR system, first determine whether the records are well-suited to CAR. In general, a CAR system works best when a query can be answered by retrieving one or two rolls of film—in other words, a transaction file. Accounts payable vendor invoices are often a good CAR application. Usually if a question arises, it is about a particular invoice rather than all of the records on that vendor. Hence, one roll of film can usually provide the needed information.

On the other hand, active personnel files are not a good CAR application, because users usually wish to review the whole file or a major portion of it. Since the file would be scattered over a number of rolls of film, a paper-based system would actually provide faster retrieval.

A second consideration is identifying carefully the fields by which the documents will be indexed. Normally you want to keep data entry to a minimum while ensuring that you can locate documents quickly. One possibility to consider is bar coding documents. Many microfilm cameras can be equipped with a bar code scanner that automatically scans the code and enters the information into the index. Thus, if purchase order numbers were bar coded, the number could automatically be entered in the index. This reduces data entry, speeds indexing, and cuts errors. The bar code error rate is approximately one in 3 million items entered, while the typical error rate for keyed-in data is one out of every 350 keystrokes.

Since a CAR system is basically a more sophisticated micrographics system, all of the issues involved in doing a micrographics needs analysis apply here.

The Micrographics Needs Analysis

Whatever type of microfilming you are considering, remember that your objective is to design an effective system, not to buy equipment. All too many organizations have problems because they don't do their homework. Instead of designing a system, they meet with two or three vendors, review the equipment shown, and make a purchase. It's not that the equipment is inferior, it just isn't the right equipment for their needs. And since no one micrographics vendor offers all types of equipment, it's quite possible that the vendors they meet with don't have the best equipment for their needs.

Your first step in the needs analysis is to identify the record categories you feel might benefit from being microfilmed. Rank them in order of priority for filming—most important to film, second most, and so on. This is necessary because one system may not meet all your needs equally well and you want to be certain that your highest-priority needs are satisfied.

Next, for each potential microfilming candidate, consider the following factors:

• *The physical characteristics of the records to be filmed.* For example, what are they—engineering drawings, checks, 8 ½- by 11-inch single sheets, or bound books? You'll need to consider their size, the weight and color of the paper, and whether both sides have to be filmed. All of these factors will affect your choice of equipment.

Also, don't forget the overall quality of the documents. Are they faded third carbons or clean originals? If the paper is brittle or very fragile, it won't be able to pass through a rotary camera. To ensure that the equipment you select can handle your records to your satisfaction, prepare a test package of examples of the poorest-quality materials that you expect to film. Have each vendor film them in your presence. (Don't leave the materials with the vendor, as you want to see what the film quality is under normal circumstances.) This type of test will prevent any unpleasant surprises after you've purchased the equipment.

• *The records' retention period.* It's stupid to film records that are near the end of their retention period. Likewise, if the records have a short retention period and are referenced infrequently, filming may not be cost-effective.

While you'll have to calculate the relative costs for your organization, a rough rule of thumb is that it's usually worthwhile to film if the records will be kept from seven to ten years. If the records are actively referenced or needed in the office area for most of their life, filming may be justified even for a shorter retention period. Also, if the records are vital, filming duplicate copies for off-site storage is cheaper than making and storing duplicate paper copies.

When converting to microfilm, start filming current records as they're created. If you begin with the backlog, you may never catch up to the present. Also, you'll realize the greatest benefits by converting current records to film and being able to take advantage of the greater productivity a film system offers during the records' period of most active use.

• *The volume of the records created.* Measure carefully, and be sure to take into account any seasonal variations. Purchase enough equipment to avoid long backlogs. If necessary, run a second shift to increase equipment utilization.

• *The update frequency of the records.* If the records are to be updated, your primary options are updatable microfiche, CAR, and jackets. With a CAR system, consider how many rolls of film must be retrieved to answer a typical query.

• *The access frequency of the records.* How frequently will the records be retrieved, how many people will handle retrieval, and how quickly will the records be needed? It's important to have adequate numbers of readers and reader-printers.

• *The number of copies of film needed.* Always plan on at least one copy in addition to the original so that the original film can be protected off-site.

• *The hard-copy requirements.* How many reader-printers will you need? Where should they be located?

• *Indexing the records.* How will documents on film be located for retrieval? If you feel CAR is the answer, be sure that the software you select will meet all your needs and be user-friendly. All of the major micrographics vendors have CAR software. Another possibility is developing your own in-house.

• *Confidentiality of records.* If you're filming highly confidential records such as personnel files, consider who will need to see the records and whether that poses a problem for the department whose records they are.

• *Turnaround criteria.* How quickly do the documents need to be converted to usable film?

• *The future.* Consider not only your current requirements but also future growth and applications. Also, using microfilm now does not preclude converting to optical disk at a later date. Many organizations are finding that they have a need for both types of media.

Four major considerations remain: the legality of microfilm, quality control, performing a cost-benefit analysis, and deciding whether to film in-house or use a service bureau. Each of these areas merits a separate discussion.

Legality of Microfilm

As already noted, microforms are generally accepted by both state and federal governments as copies admissible as evidence in courts of law. The primary basis is statutory, under the Uniform Photographic Copies of Business and Public Records as Evidence Act (UPA) and the Uniform Rules of Evidence (URE). States that have not adopted one or both of these pieces of legislation have adopted similar statutes addressing the legality of microfilm.

In addition, most government and regulatory agencies have established policies and statutes in favor of accepting microfilmed records. However, some agencies, such as the Internal Revenue Service, do have specific requirements that filmed records must meet to be accepted. Skupsky's *Recordkeeping Requirements* (see References) has an extensive discussion of the statutes governing the legal acceptance of microfilm.

Note that the legal acceptability of COM is not an issue; with COM, the microfilm itself is the original record and hence admissible.

Quality Control

Micrographics is a highly technical area. And as in many technical fields, quality control is an essential consideration. The four basic quality issues in micrographics are residual thiosulfate, resolution, density, and film inspection and legibility.

1. *Residual thiosulfate.* If you've ever developed film, you're probably familiar with the term *hypo.* Hypo, or sodium thiosulfate, is the chemical commonly used in the developing process to "fix" film. If too much thiosulfate remains on the film after it is developed, the thiosulfate eventually causes the film to deteriorate. Therefore, a chemical test—normally the methylene blue test—must be used to check the residue level. Note that this test only applies to wet silver (silver gelatin) microfilm, as thiosulfate is not used in developing other types of microfilm.

2. *Resolution.* The second quality control area—resolution—measures the micrographics system's capability to separate fine detail. A chart is filmed, and the patterns are examined under a microscope to determine the smallest pattern in which lines can be distinguished both horizontally and vertically.

3. *Density.* Density is the opacity or degree of darkness of the "black" portion of the film—the background on negative film. Density is measured by a special piece of equipment called a densitometer.

4. *Film inspection and legibility.* The last major quality control area is the simplest yet most important. It requires no chemical tests or elaborate equipment, just a reader. Film inspection and legibility means just that: visually inspecting each image of the film to check that it is properly positioned and legible. This should *always* be done before the originals are destroyed.

Admittedly, this last item sounds like a simple, obvious precaution. Yet perhaps because it is so obvious, it is sometimes neglected—with disastrous results. For example, several years ago, when two major stock brokerage firms merged, large masses of documents were quickly filmed by temporary workers and then destroyed.

It was subsequently discovered that one temporary employee had filmed documents for three days with no film in the camera. As you might imagine, the firms' customers were not too pleased when they read the story on the front page of *The Wall Street Journal*. A simple quality control check would have prevented the problem.

One other quality control item: If drawings to scale are being filmed and will later be restored to their original size, be sure to check the reduction scale of the camera.

The specific ANSI standards on micrographics quality control are cited in the References.

The Cost-Benefit Analysis

A key factor in deciding whether or not to film records is cost justification. You'll need to compare the costs of your current operation with those of filming the records. I recommend that you do the analysis for five years; by the end of that period, you'll undoubtedly be upgrading equipment or switching to a different technology.

To determine the cost of your present operation, consider:

1. The cost of the space occupied by the active records (don't forget to include aisle space as well as the actual square footage occupied by the filing cabinets)

2. The cost of storing the inactive records
3. The cost of the time spent processing, handling, and filing the records under your current system
4. The cost of additional filing equipment and supplies

The cost of the film system would include:

1. The cost of all necessary equipment (you may want to consider leasing as an alternative)
2. The cost for film, processing, and supplies
3. The cost of the time spent in document preparation, filming, and checking the film
4. The cost of the time spent retrieving and using the film
5. Maintenance contracts for the micrographics equipment

Of course, you may decide to microfilm records for other than monetary reasons, such as the need for vital records protection and whether your company can continue functioning with a paper-based system.

In-House Operation, or Service Bureau?

One final decision related to using micrographics is whether to film in-house or have a service bureau perform the work. Of course, part of the decision is financial: For the volume of work you have, which type of operation will be cheaper?

Another key consideration is turnaround time. If a service bureau cannot meet your needs in this area, you will be forced to go in-house.

If you do use a service bureau, you may still want to prepare documents for filming in-house. Labor-intensive tasks such as removing staples and paper clips, taping tears, and purging duplicates may be performed more cheaply in-house than by a service bureau.

Even if you do the bulk of your filming in-house, you may want to use a service bureau for specialty work where your volume does not justify in-house filming. For example, you might not have enough engineering drawings to justify acquiring a large planetary camera. Service bureaus are also useful for conversions, backlogs, and, as already discussed, COM.

Or you may decide to film in-house but have your film processed by a service bureau. In addition to freeing yourself from the need to acquire processing equipment and train staff in this area, you also avoid problems with the proper disposal of the chemicals involved in processing.

Even if you plan to do your filming in-house, it's still a good idea to investigate service bureaus in your area. First of all, you can learn a great deal about microfilming by visiting service bureaus. After all, filming is their business. Second, you might unexpectedly have a need for a service bureau later on. If you're already familiar with the ones in your area, selecting the right one will be much easier.

As you can see from this chapter, micrographics is a highly technical area. To cover it in depth would require a book at least this size. Thus, this chapter must serve as an overview. You may want to consult some of the reference works cited in the References. AIIM (see Records Management Resources) is also an excellent source for more information.

11

Document Imaging
Optical Disk Systems

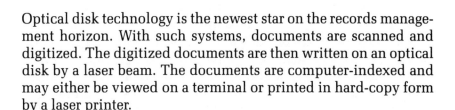

Optical disk technology is the newest star on the records management horizon. With such systems, documents are scanned and digitized. The digitized documents are then written on an optical disk by a laser beam. The documents are computer-indexed and may either be viewed on a terminal or printed in hard-copy form by a laser printer.

System Types

Although there are three types of optical disk systems available, I will be discussing only one—WORM. WORM stands for Write Once Read Many times. With a WORM system, documents can be added to the disk until it is filled. Documents cannot be removed from the disk once they are written on it. These two features make WORM particularly attractive from a records management standpoint. The disk can be added to just as you would add to a file folder. And the inability to remove documents from the disk protects file integrity and helps provide legal credibility.

The other two types of systems available now are CD-ROM and erasable optical disks. With a CD-ROM system, a master disk is made, then duplicates are prepared for users. Users cannot add or delete information from the disk. CD-ROM's current primary application is as an alternative publishing medium for databases and reference books.

Erasable optical disks function similarly to magnetic disk drives on a computer. Data can be removed, altered, and replaced. While there are many benefits to this technology within the computer systems environment, the ability to remove and replace documents raises the issues of file integrity and legal credibility.

Advantages of a WORM System

Optical disk technology provides a number of benefits to the user. These include:

• *Highly compact storage.* At the time of this writing, a 12-inch optical disk typically holds approximately thirty thousand 8 ½- by 11-inch pages on each side, while a 5 ¼-inch disk holds approximately eight thousand letter-size pages per side. In other words, one 12-inch disk could hold the equivalent of approximately twenty rolls of microfilm. Impressive as these numbers are, disk capacity is constantly being enhanced.

• *Integration of document management, data management, and text processing.* Many optical disk systems permit data to be input by a variety of means: scanning of hard copy or microfilm, keyboard entry, and transfer from the computer system. Also depending on the system, the user can review both document images and computer data simultaneously through "windows" on the terminal screen.

• *Computer indexing of data.* Depending on the software used, documents can be indexed and retrieved by a wide range of fields.

• *DRAW (Direct Read After Write).* Since disks, unlike microfilm, do not require processing, the documents are available immediately after they are scanned, indexed, and written to the disk. In practice though, many organizations scan and index the documents during the day but write them to disk after hours. In the interim, the documents are stored in a file server or buffer so that all of the disk drives will be available during the day for user retrieval needs.

• *Rapid retrieval.* Users can retrieve documents at their terminals without going to a file room or pulling rolls of film and inserting them in a reader. The actual retrieval speed depends on such factors as the number of users, the number of disk drives, the size of the disks, and whether the desired disk is already in the drive. However, normal retrieval time is one minute or less.

• *Concurrent access to data by multiple users.* With a networked system, multiple users can review the same document simultaneously. This eliminates problems with checked-out records and allows users in different offices to discuss the same record over the phone.

• *Improvements in document flow and transmittal.* Documents can be routed electronically from one individual to another. This, of course, is considerably faster than transmitting paper and eliminates the risk of the document's being lost. Thus, insurance claims or credit card applications can be transmitted for processing electronically within the organization.

• *Ease of updating files.* Files can be added to indefinitely. However, since retrieval speed is faster if all of the documents in a file are on the same side of the same disk, you may want to spread files over several disk sides instead of filling up one side completely. Thus, personnel records for employees A–D might be on disk A, side 1, E–H on disk A, side 2, I–M on disk B, side 1, and so on, even though you could have fit A–M on one disk side. This way, as new material comes in, it can be written to the appropriate disk, thus speeding retrieval of the complete file.

• *No special environmental protection needed.* Because the disks are hermetically sealed, you do not have to store them in a climate-controlled facility. The longevity of disks is increasing steadily. As of this writing, many vendors are guaranteeing twenty- to thirty-year lives for their disks. At the end of that period, the data can be written to another disk if there is a need to still retain it. And by that time, disk life should be considerably longer.

Other Considerations

As you can see, optical disk technology offers a number of exciting benefits. However, five other factors that must be considered are:

1. *Cost of the system.* While the prices of small stand-alone systems have been coming down steadily and are now less expensive than comparable micrographics installations, large networked systems still represent a major capital investment that can run into millions of dollars. I discuss doing a cost-benefit analysis later in this chapter.

2. *Lack of industry standardization.* While microfilm produced on one vendor's equipment can normally be read on another vendor's system, the same is not true of optical disks. When you select a vendor, you are basically locked into that vendor's system. (Data could be rewritten to another vendor's disks and systems, but it's not a simple process.)

There's currently a great deal of debate about whether or not lack of standards is a problem. After all, companies typically commit themselves to a primary vendor for their main computer systems, and no one expects to be able to load a DEC disk on an IBM drive and read it. There has been some movement toward standardization of 5 ¼-inch disks, and it's conceivable that eventually we may have the same type of compatibility with the smaller optical disk systems as we do with personal computers.

3. *Legal acceptability of disk images.* Some experts argue that the statutes that make microfilm legally acceptable as evidence apply as well to optical disks—that an optical disk image is a durable, accurate copy of the original. Others argue the reverse—that an optical disk image is not a copy but a re-creation of the document after digitization. Another issue is that although documents cannot be altered after they are written to disk, they can be altered after scanning when they are held in the file server. Of course, paper files and microfilm are not immune to tampering either: A document can be removed from a paper file with no one being the wiser, and an incriminating note can be whited out or erased before filming.

However, the issue here is not logic but legal acceptability. At this time, federal statutes do not specifically address the issue, although some federal agencies have made rulings. Certain states have passed laws saying optical disk images are legally acceptable, but at least one state has ruled against the use of disk. Eventually the issue will be resolved in favor of optical disk—after all, the federal government has invested more in systems than anyone else.

But what will happen in the future doesn't help you now. Your legal department will need to decide whether hard copy can be disposed of after documents are scanned. Some organizations are disposing of the hard copy while others are maintaining it off-site in case it should be required for litigation. Until the statutes become clearer, this is an area I would leave in the hands of legal counsel.

4. *System life span.* One reason some government bodies have so far rejected optical disks is their concern about the ability to access records in future years. While microfilm readers are relatively generic and will continue to be available, optical disk commits you to a specific system. Therefore, a key consideration is whether equipment to support that system will continue to be available.

With systems with a large number of installations, equipment undoubtedly will be available or conversions will be possible. But if the vendor from whom you purchase has only a few installations and then goes out of business, you might have serious problems.

5. *Slowness of scanning.* Despite steady improvements, it still takes much longer to scan and digitize a document than to film it. This means you'll need more scanners and more staff to support them. I discuss scanners in the next section.

System Components

Because it is both an imaging system and a computer system, an optical disk system requires a number of components. These include:

• *Scanners.* The first step in converting a document to disk is scanning. Scanners come in a wide range of models, from tabletop units for scanning letter- and legal-size documents to large units for scanning engineering drawings. There are also microfilm scanners. Most units have automatic document feeds, and some can scan both sides of a page simultaneously.

With scanners, the two most important issues you need to know about are scanning resolution and speed. Scanning resolution refers to the number of dots or pixels per inch at which the material is scanned. Higher resolutions improve image quality, but they increase the amount of space the document takes up on the disk; this lowers disk capacity and slows scanning speed.

Scanning at 200 pixels per inch produces legible copies of office records in good condition; 300 pixels per inch produces material equivalent to laser printer output; at 400 pixels per inch, the copy closely resembles the original. Most organizations use 200 pixels per inch and rescan documents at a higher resolution as needed.

Speed depends on the scanner's capabilities and the scanning resolution. The amount of material on the document is also important: It takes much longer to scan a single-spaced form with small type than to scan a double-spaced half-page memo. So don't simply rely on a vendor's estimate of the number of pages per minute. You'll need to test the equipment thoroughly with the kinds of documents you'll be inputting to get an accurate estimate of the system's speed.

• *User workstations.* Systems range from one-person stand-alone units (see photograph) with a single workstation to large installations with thousands of workstations networked together. While existing PC workstations may be adequate for casual or infrequent uses, major users of the system will need high-resolution workstations so that they can view documents clearly and take full advantage of the system's capabilities. Many systems permit "windowing," which allows users to view several documents at once or to view both a document image and data from the mainframe at the same time. Often documents can be shrunk or expanded in size.

• *Software.* Software is, of course, a critical system component. In most cases, you'll be working with software developed

An optical disk workstation.

Courtesy Eastman Kodak Company.

by the vendor, although it may be customized for your organization. Just as with a CAR system, you'll need to determine how you want to index documents for easy retrieval. If documents are to be routed through the organization, that will be another key consideration.

• *Buffers or file servers.* File servers are the links that make the whole system run smoothly. Documents are held in the servers until they are written to the disk. When documents are retrieved, they pass through the servers again. Therefore, having an adequate number of servers is essential if retrieval speed is to meet user expectations.

• *The CPU (central processing unit) or host computer.* The computer that supports the entire system can be anything from a PC to a mainframe. Smaller systems tend to be PC-based while the larger ones are tied to the corporate mainframe.

• *The optical disk.* I've already mentioned that disk size and capacity are closely related. While 3 ½-, 8-, and 14-inch disks are used with some systems, the vast majority use either 5 ¼- or 12-inch disks. Key issues are the number of records you need to maintain on-line in the system and retrieval speed. It is faster for the system to search the smaller disk. On the other hand, less data can be available on-line with the smaller disks, as they hold less and the jukeboxes that contain them hold fewer disks.

• *Disk drives and jukeboxes.* With a small system that has only one disk drive, an operator loads the appropriate disk into the drive to search for a document. With a larger system, a jukebox (see photograph) automatically loads the appropriate disk into a drive when a document is requested. Depending on the unit, a jukebox can hold anywhere from 16 to 300 disks and may have from one to 6 disk drives inside. Currently, most drives are single-sided, and the disk must be turned if the other side is to be accessed; however, double-sided drives are now beginning to enter the marketplace.

• *Laser printers.* Hard copies are produced by a laser printer. You will need to know the speed of the printer, the resolution or sharpness of its output, and the size(s) of paper it will accommodate. Again, it is important to test output quality on your documents. One organization discovered after purchasing a system

Two optical disk jukeboxes.

Courtesy Eastman Kodak Company.

that while notes in the margins appeared on the workstation screen, the printer "clipped" them off because it didn't print all the way out to the edge of the paper.

Design Considerations

When you talk with organizations that have optical disk systems in place, you hear reactions ranging from great satisfaction to complete dissatisfaction. When you talk further with these companies, a pattern emerges. The organizations that are happy with their systems did their homework carefully; the unhappy ones didn't. They thought throwing hardware at their records problems would make the problems go away.

Some of the issues you need to consider if you're thinking about implementing an optical disk system are:

• *Both its initial scope and how it will need to grow.* If you'll eventually need a large system, be sure the one you select can be expanded. For example, if you expect to need a jukebox in the future, be sure the system can be upgraded with one.

• *Identification of the system's primary objective.* Is your goal to improve the storage and retrieval of documents or to simplify work flow and document transmission? Different systems are better for different applications.

A stand-alone optical disk system.

Courtesy Tab Products Company.

• *Document flow.* As a first step, chart the flow of relevant documents through the organization. What changes in that flow do you want? The flowchart will be one of the most important documents in the system development process.

• *Physical characteristics of documents to be input.* Many of the same issues involved in a micrographics needs analysis come into play here. For example: Can you use an automatic document feed? How much document preparation is required prior to scanning?

However, there are additional concerns unique to optical disk technology. I've already discussed scanning resolution levels. Another factor is redesigning forms and other materials to reduce the amount of disk space they occupy. Graphics consume considerably more disk space than typed text, so you'll want to keep to a minimum the amount of artwork used on forms.

• *Disk clustering and disk retention.* As discussed earlier, you'll want to allocate disk space so that, if possible, all the documents in a particular file will be located on the same disk. And since documents cannot be removed from a disk, all of the documents on a disk will have to have the same retention period. This, too, may affect how you group materials on the disks.

• *Conversion of old files.* Converting older files tends to be extremely costly and labor-intensive. If files do need to be converted because they are still active, decide whether to do the conversion in-house or hire a service bureau. Keep in mind that scanning and indexing documents are skilled tasks. As many companies have learned the hard way, you can't simply bring in temporaries with no training and expect satisfactory results.

• *System backup and archiving.* Although disks are not vulnerable to temperature or humidity changes, they certainly can be destroyed in a fire or other disaster. What will you use to back up the system off-site: duplicate disks? magnetic tape? hard copy? microfilm? Some systems are easier to back up than others.

• *Ability to interface with your existing system.* If you're considering a large system, mainframe compatibility is a key issue. If you have existing computer indexes or an existing microfilm system, will you need to merge these into the new system? If so, how?

A workstation for digitizing microfilm.

Courtesy Eastman Kodak Company.

An integrated optical disk and micrographics system.

• *The vendor's financial stability and prior experience.* Because you will be totally locked into a particular vendor's system, be sure that the vendor you choose has staying power. Several vendors have already gone out of business, leaving users in awkward positions. And even if someone buys out the vendor, the rules of the game may change. One company, whose vendor was bought out, found out that the new owners of the company would not honor the warranty if the equipment were moved to a new location!

You'll probably also want a vendor with considerable experience, although some companies opt to be "beta sites" or experimental locations. There are often substantial cost incentives for being a guinea pig, but there are also substantial risks. If you're going with a start-up vendor, proceed with caution.

The Cost-Benefit Analysis

In spite of their high costs, many companies that have installed large optical disk systems feel financially justified in doing so. True, financial considerations are not always predominant: For some, functioning with paper or microfilm is no longer viable; for others, more rapid customer service has been the deciding factor. However, even if monetary factors are not the only basis for your decision to go this route, they certainly should be a major consideration. Therefore, you must do a cost-benefit analysis.

First, quantify the number of documents received, processed, stored, and retrieved each day and list the average number of pages per document. Be sure to consider any daily or seasonal variations, and, if possible, quantify the number of misfiles—an optical disk system should virtually eliminate misfiles, which can mean a substantial labor savings.

Just as with a micrographics needs analysis, you'll need to identify all the costs of your existing system (see Chapter 10). Also consider photocopying costs—an optical disk system can reduce substantially the number of photocopies and duplicates, as users can reference records directly on their terminals.

Then, in addition to the cost of the equipment for the optical disk system you select, consider both start-up costs and operating costs.

Start-Up Costs

- System installation
- Training of personnel
- Conversion of old documents (if appropriate)
- Modification of existing forms and procedures to accommodate the new system

Operating Costs

- Equipment maintenance contracts
- Disks (don't forget backup copies)
- Space occupied by the equipment
- Time spent scanning, indexing, retrieving, and printing documents
- Paper and printer supplies
- If documents are not being destroyed after they are written to disk, the cost of storing them off-site

The Records Manager's Role in the Decision-Making Process

Obviously, a decision of this magnitude is not made by one person. The systems or data processing department will have significant input; so will the potential users of the system. However, it is essential that you, the records manager, have some input into the decision. Since records are being created, all of the records management considerations apply, including:

- Records retention
- Records backup and vital records protection
- Legal considerations, including whether the originals need be retained
- Long-term perspective—not just how the system will work now, but how it will work when it's fully loaded
- Indexing of information for easy retrieval
- Physical issues connected with document conversion

Many of the system problems I've learned about occurred because the records management issues listed above were not considered. For example, at one seminar, two individuals from the human resources department of a major corporation announced that they had installed an optical disk system for benefit and pension records. Their major goal was to eliminate hard copies of these records. When I inquired if their legal counsel had approved the destruction of the originals after scanning, I learned that they were not even aware that destroying the originals might pose a legal problem.

Computer Output Laser Disk

We have primarily been discussing source document optical disk imaging. However, computer printouts can also be written to optical disk. Thus, instead of COM, we have COLD (computer output laser disk). And this is one cold that benefits its users, as both space savings and retrieval speed exceed those provided by COM. And, just as with COM, there is no issue of legal acceptability because the COLD image is an original document.

Optical Disk or Micrographics?

The decision whether to implement an optical disk system or a micrographics system is a complex one. An optical disk system provides faster retrieval of records and allows several users to access a file simultaneously. On the other hand, scanning documents is considerably slower than filming them.

An optical disk system allows you to combine access to document images, computer files, and text processing in one system. And if files must be added to over an extended period of time, retrieval is much faster than with micrographics.

Microfilm is a longer-lived but more fragile medium. The legal acceptability of microfilm is well-established; that of an optical disk system is still being debated. For small single-user systems, optical disk is cheaper; for large multiuser systems, film is cheaper but does less.

Each organization must base its decision on its own needs and requirements. And, of course, one possible decision is to do nothing at this time. Many companies are waiting until optical disk is a more mature technology before taking the plunge. Even more so than with micrographics, implementing an optical disk system is a complex and highly technical process. Also the technology is advancing daily.

I've tried in this chapter to provide a thorough overview of such systems while avoiding statements that would be out of date before the book was published. The References list additional resources. Also, as with micrographics, AIIM is an excellent resource for current information.

12

Forms Management— An Integral Part of Records Management

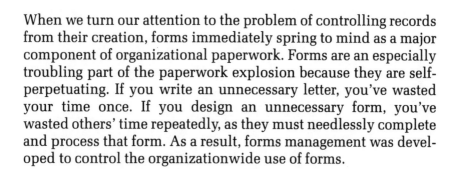

When we turn our attention to the problem of controlling records from their creation, forms immediately spring to mind as a major component of organizational paperwork. Forms are an especially troubling part of the paperwork explosion because they are self-perpetuating. If you write an unnecessary letter, you've wasted your time once. If you design an unnecessary form, you've wasted others' time repeatedly, as they must needlessly complete and process that form. As a result, forms management was developed to control the organizationwide use of forms.

What Is Forms Management?

Forms management involves analyzing the user's needs to determine what form (if any) is needed, designing the best possible one to meet those needs, and finally monitoring all forms used by the organization to ensure maximum efficiency in ordering, stocking, and distribution. The overall objectives of the process are to increase organizational efficiency and productivity and to save money in both the production and use of forms.

Forms management achieves these objectives through the following actions:

- Eliminating unnecessary forms, unnecessary copies of forms, and unnecessary items on forms
- Consolidating forms that serve similar purposes
- Preventing unnecessary new forms and unnecessary revisions to existing forms
- Designing forms for maximum effectiveness
- Ensuring proper reproduction, stocking, and distribution of forms

Relationship Between Forms Management and Records Management

I firmly believe that forms management belongs under the jurisdiction of records management, since records management is concerned with the entire life cycle of a record from creation to destruction. A form is simply a type of record, albeit a repetitive one, that can waste considerable organizational resources unless managed properly.

However, I am well aware that not all records managers have forms management under their jurisdiction. In some organizations, it is a separate and equal function; in others, it falls under the jurisdiction of systems and procedures, printing, or purchasing.

But even if forms management is not part of your responsibilities, you need a working knowledge of this area for two reasons. First, as you've probably already noticed, records management uses quite a few forms, and you want to be sure they are properly designed, produced, and stocked.

Second, the company's forms can have a major impact on your job, especially in the area of document imaging: Forms printed on very thin paper are difficult to scan or film; whether or not the paper is colored and which copy of a multipart form you receive affects filming or scanning; and scanning artwork, logos, and other such decorations on forms uses up considerable disk space. Hence, it's in your best interest to coordinate efforts closely with your company's forms designer if the responsibility is not under your jurisdiction.

Where to Begin

If you have been given responsibility for forms management, but either there is no program in place or the one you've got is dormant, you must do one of two things. The first is simply to take over the forms ordering and reordering functions and put the new program into effect gradually by consolidating, revising, or eliminating existing forms when they are due for reorder and by designing effective new forms as they are needed. Because this alternative will achieve your dual objectives of increased efficiency and reduced expense gradually, it is less desirable than your other option. This second alternative requires a major initial effort, but you reap the benefits much more quickly. You begin by surveying and classifying all corporate forms. Then, starting with the major problem areas revealed by the survey, you consolidate, redesign, and eliminate forms as needed.

Conducting a Forms Survey

A forms survey is much simpler to conduct than a records inventory because you don't have to visit each department to collect the forms. Instead, you can send out a memo signed by an appropriate top executive (see Exhibit 12-1) introducing the program and listing the information you will need about each form.

Classifying the Forms

Once you've collected this huge mass of paper, your next job is to organize it. This involves setting up three different types of files: numeric, functional, and specifications. The numeric file will be a paper filing system; the functional and specifications files may

Exhibit 12-1.   Example of a memo introducing the forms survey.

To: All department heads   Date: _____

From: *{name}*

     {Company name} is instituting a forms management program to increase our forms' effectiveness, reduce their cost, and eliminate unnecessary paperwork. When the program is fully implemented, our new forms management department, headed by *{name}*, will be responsible for designing and ordering all forms.

     The first step in the program is collecting copies of all forms now in use. Please send three copies of each form your department uses to *{name, department}* by *{date—usually two weeks later}*. On one copy of each form, write the following information:

         Your department name
         Whether the form is filled in by machine or by hand
         Where your department obtains the form
         Number of copies of the form your department uses annually
         Cost of the form, if known

     Even if another department uses the same form, you should still submit three copies. And remember that a form is any standardized, preprinted means of collecting information, including labels, checks, envelopes, letterhead, questionnaires, and standard contracts.

     If you have any questions about the program, please call *{name}* at *{extension}*.

---

be paper files, card files, or a combined computer database listing all forms and classifying them both by function and by specifications. You might opt for one of the commercial forms management software packages. There are packages for forms design, indexing, and monitoring inventory levels, as well as packages that integrate all of the forms management functions.

The Numeric File

As its name implies, the numeric file is arranged by form number. This historical file contains all available information about the form—e.g., the specifications sheet, order requests, and purchase order or print shop requisitions—as well as several copies of the form and any other pertinent information.

Of course, if no forms numbering system exists, you'll have to develop one. The most effective systems tend to be the simplest. You're not trying to capsulize all relevant information about the form in the number, you're simply providing a unique identifier for that form.

Consecutive numbering is easiest and generally works well for companies having up to 3,000 forms. You assign each form a four-digit number, beginning with 0001. Since forms are revised frequently, add the letter A for the first printed version (e.g., 1099-A). When the form is revised, the number changes to 1099-B, and so on. Instead of an alpha code, you could use the revision date (e.g., 1099-6/90), but that makes the number longer. Also, users may feel that a perfectly good form is out of date because its date is not that current.

Another forms numbering system is particularly effective for organizations that are diversified or have several thousand forms. In these cases, the form number can be prefaced with an alpha code that indicates whether the form is for use overall or only within a particular division. For example, CH1044-A would be a form used in the chemicals division, while CP1044-A would be for overall corporate use.

The same system can also be used to indicate the particular *function* or subject the form pertains to, such as HUM for human resources or MKT for marketing. However, linking the form number to a specific *department* can create problems. If the organization is restructured, the form numbers may no longer match the departments. Also, some departments feel possessive about their forms. They then discourage other departments from using their forms by insisting the forms be designed exclusively for their needs.

The Functional File

The functional file groups forms by what they do. This type of file helps consolidate or eliminate forms that serve similar purposes. It also helps prevent the creation of unnecessary new forms.

Functional filing systems can be set up on two or three levels. The first level is the form's subject; the second and third levels subdivide that subject. For over 2,000 forms, you'll probably prefer a three-level system. For smaller quantities, a two-level system should suffice.

With either system, the first level denotes the form's subject—e.g., "customers," "employment," "fixed assets," or "insurance." The second level, the modifier, amplifies or explains what is done to the subject—e.g., "application for" or "change of." With a three-level system, the third level, indicating what is done, uses an action verb—e.g., "to authorize," "to request," or "to order."

Here's a sample group of functional files set up on three levels.

Employment	Position	To establish
Employment	Position	To change
Employment	Position	To eliminate
Records	Microfilming	To request
Records	Microfilming	To approve
Records	Microfilming	To check
Records	Retention schedule	To change

The functional categories would be reviewed for possible consolidation. For example, one form might be used to establish, change, or eliminate an employment position, or to request and approve records for microfilming. When new forms are requested, the function file is checked to see if an existing form either meets or can be adapted to meet the need.

The Specifications File

The specifications file classifies forms by their physical characteristics or construction. Typical categories are "envelopes," "continuous forms," "snap-out forms," "self-adhesive labels," and "letterhead." A form could conceivably fit in more than one category, as would self-adhesive mailing labels in a continuous roll.

The specifications file helps you reduce printing costs by grouping similar orders. For example, when you order self-adhesive shipping labels, you can check to see if any other self-adhesive labels are close to their reorder points. If they are, grouping the orders may reduce the printing setup charge and result in a high-volume discount.

Forms Analysis and Design

Forms analysis and design are two major ongoing activities in any forms management program. Analysis identifies the user's needs that must be met by the form, while design uses the information collected from analysis to develop the best possible form. Normally one individual, a forms analyst, performs both the analysis and design functions for a particular group of forms.

Analysis

The analyst obtains answers to the following questions regarding the form's content, usage, and physical features.

Content

1. *What information does the user* need *to collect on the form?* Note the emphasis on *need.* The user should be able to justify every item he or she wants on the form. It's also a good idea to have the user indicate which information is most important.

2. *Can any of the questions on the form have multiple-choice answers?* Listing all possible answers saves time by reducing the amount of writing. Multiple choices also speed data compilation, as less handwriting has to be deciphered and responses are channeled into a limited number of categories. Remember, you can always use "other: _____" for situations not covered by the given categories.

Usage

1. *How many copies of the form will be used in a year?* You don't want to spend a great deal of time designing a low-usage form (under 500 copies a year); it simply isn't cost-effective. In

these cases, you could ask the user to prepare a rough draft of the form, which you then polish and incorporate into the system. If only one department uses such a form, you may want to make that department responsible for storing it and notifying you when the reorder point is reached.

2. *Who will be completing the form?* What's their educational background and level of familiarity with the material on the form? For example, customers completing the form at home need very comprehensive, simple instructions.

3. *Where will the form be completed?* The conditions under which the form must be completed may affect its physical design. For example, a shop supervisor may need a book of maintenance forms that can be stuck in a pocket, while a clerk sitting at a desk can work well with an 8 ½- by 11-inch form.

4. *Who needs copies of the form?* You want to keep the number of copies to a minimum, as extra copies have a habit of creeping into files and records storage. Also they add cost.

5. *Does the form relate to other forms, either as a source of information for them or as a result of them?* If it does, get samples of the other forms and explore the possibility of consolidation. Even if you can't consolidate the forms, you do want to design them as a system so that they complement each other.

6. *Is the form a source document for computer input?* If so, it must be developed so that data can be transferred easily. You'll need to know how many spaces are available for each data item, the order in which items will be entered into the computer system, and what, if any, data will not be entered. Ideally, the computer system and the form are designed together, but in reality, one often precedes the other.

Physical Features

1. *Will the form be microfilmed or scanned optically?* Making sure it is the original or first copy that will be scanned or filmed improves image quality. Remember, weight and color of paper may make a difference. If the document will be scanned, eliminate any superfluous artwork or graphics that will waste disk space.

2. *Does the form have any special size requirements, and how will it be filed?* Must it fit in a card file or into a binder?

3. *How long will the form be kept?* Any new document you create should have a retention period assigned. If the form will be retained for many years and will not be filmed or scanned, you may need to use a better-than-normal grade of paper to ensure the form's longevity.

Design

Once the analyst has collected all of the above information, he or she is ready to prepare a rough draft of the form. The first step is to sort all the desired information into logical groups, such as by customer name, address, and phone number. Next, he or she arranges these groups in a logical order—logical, that is, for the person who completes and/or processes the form.

Finally, the forms analyst prepares a rough draft, which should be photocopied and the copies given to the user for testing. Testing is the most important step in the whole process and should be performed for every new or extensively revised form. Even if the user tells you the form looks perfect, test it. Only testing in real-world situations will let you know if the form really works. Too many companies have learned this lesson the hard way.

Forms design is not difficult or complicated—not, that is, if you follow these rules. They will help you create forms that are efficient, economical, and attractive.

1. *Use the box or ULC (upper left caption) design,* as shown in the top example in Exhibit 12-2. This design enables you to fit more items into less space, speeds completion if the form will be typed or filled in on a computer by reducing the amount of spacing and tabbing, and reduces the chance of misplaced information.

Whenever possible, line up the caption boxes as shown in the top example in Exhibit 12-2 (see entries for employee number, home telephone, and zip code). This reduces the number of tab stops needed and is visually more appealing.

Exhibit 12-2.   Acceptable and unacceptable caption designs.

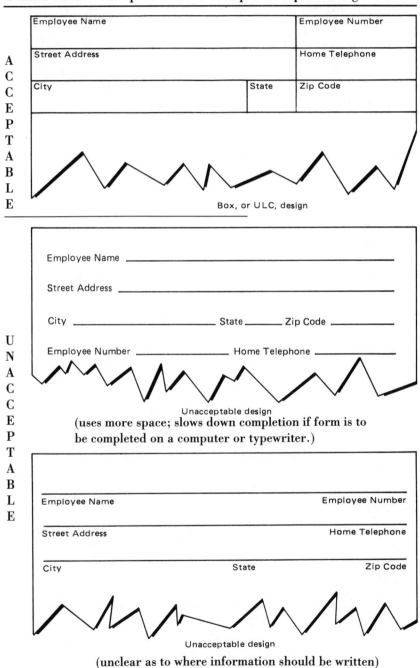

2. *Use clear, descriptive captions.* Words like *name, number,* and *date* may mean one thing to you and another to the person completing the form. For example, on an insurance form, *date* might refer either to when the form was completed or to when the accident occurred.

3. *Write questions in a multiple-choice format whenever possible.* To avoid misunderstandings, put the check box (☐) in front of the item, not behind it, and space accordingly.

Acceptable: ☐ Excellent   ☐ Good   ☐ Fair   ☐Poor
Unacceptable: Excellent☐   Good☐   Fair☐   Poor☐

4. *Leave ample space for writing information.* If the forms are to be completed on a computer or typewriter, align the lines to match the equipment's spacing. For horizontal lines, allow 2 inches for the first ten characters and 1 inch for every seven to eight additional characters. If you don't know how long a name will be, allow at least 3 inches. And if the data will be entered in a computer, use tick marks, not boxes, to indicate the number of spaces in the data field. (Boxes make it difficult to transfer data accurately.)

Acceptable: └┴┴┴┴┴┴┴┴┴┴┴┴┴┴┴┴┴┘
Unacceptable: ☐☐☐☐☐☐☐☐☐☐☐☐☐☐☐☐☐☐

If you want people to write comments on the form, draw horizontal lines for them to write on. Lines are better for motivating users to write than a large blank space. They also help control extremely large or small handwriting, thus making the form easier to read.

5. *Always put the form number in the same place.* There are four schools of thought as to the preferred spot: upper left corner, lower left, upper right, lower right. It really doesn't matter which you choose as long as you're consistent.

6. *Allow at least a ⅜-inch margin all around the form and a ¾-inch margin on the left-hand side if the form is to be three-hole-punched.* The margin serves several purposes. First, print-

ing presses do not usually print to the edges, and extending the lines through "bleeding" is expensive. Second, margins increase the form's readability. Third, if the form will be scanned, information won't be lost because the scanner doesn't read to the edge of the page.

7. *Use a serif typeface for text and lengthy instructions and a sans serif typeface for captions, headings, and short instructions.* Serifs are the angled lines, or "feet," extending from letters (the text for this book is set in a serif typeface). Helvetica and Univers are commonly used sans serif types, while Century is a popular serif type. Serif type is easier to read in text because the serifs break the monotony, but sans serif is cleaner and more effective for headings, captions, and other short items.

8. *Write clear, concise instructions.* If several steps are involved, number and list them. For example:

To report a theft:

1. Complete sections 1, 2, 3, and 5 of this form.
2. Send the white and yellow copies of this form to your insurance agent, along with a copy of the policy report.
3. Keep the green copy for your records.

Ideally, the form should be self-explanatory so that users don't have to refer to a procedures manual to find out how to complete it. If the instructions are too long or too complex to fit on the form itself, print them on a thin cover sheet that can be torn off and referred to while the form is being completed. If the forms are contained in a book, you may want to print the instructions on the inside cover. But never print the instructions on the back of the form; if you do, they will be overlooked. In any case, it's very frustrating to keep having to flip the form over to read them.

9. *If a form is multipart, be sure to indicate the proper distribution order either in the instructions or at the bottom of the form.* It's also a good idea to use different colors for each copy. If you will be microfilming the form, design it so that the copy to be filmed will be white.

10. *Use standard-size paper whenever possible to reduce costs and minimize waste.* Standard sizes are those that can be cut evenly from a 17- by 22-inch sheet of paper. For example, four 8 ½- by 11-inch pages can be cut evenly from such a sheet. Other standard sizes are 17″ × 11″, 8 ½″ × 7⅓″, 8 ½″ × 5½″, and 4 ¼″ by 5 ½″.

11. *Consider using chemical carbonless paper for multi-copy forms.** One big advantage of such paper is that you can usually print the forms in-house, while carbon-interleaved or snap-out forms usually require the services of an outside printer. Forms printed on chemical carbonless paper take less storage space, are cheaper to ship, and are generally preferred by users because they are less messy. However, depending on the quantity ordered, carbon sets can produce more copies and may cost less. And some users report allergies to chemical carbonless paper— apparently a reaction to the formaldehyde released from the tiny dye capsules contained in the paper.

Forms Control

It's not enough to design the best possible forms. You also need to control the entire forms process. The forms manager must work as a team not only with users of the forms but with the print shop, the purchasing manager, and the supply room to ensure that forms are printed quickly, efficiently, and economically and that they are in stock when needed.

The Printing Decision

The decision as to whether to print in-house or go outside should be based on your in-house print shop's ability to do the work in terms of both equipment and time, as well as the comparative cost.

One option you may want to consider is having an outside

---

* Sometimes incorrectly referred to as NCR (no carbon required) paper. In reality NCR is the trademark for Appleton Paper's brand of chemical carbonless paper.

firm provide a complete forms management program. A number of vendors can provide programs tailored to your company's individual needs, but typically they include:

- Design of all forms
- Warehousing of the forms
- A complete inventory control service
- Delivery of the forms to the client as needed

Depending on your in-house capabilities and your forms volume, you may find such a program to be cost-effective. The major advantage is that it provides you with a complete, professional forms management program that requires much less effort on your part than staffing an in-house function. The major drawback is that you become totally dependent on an outside supplier. If problems develop, extricating yourself from the relationship can be difficult and time-consuming, so if you are considering such a program, choose your vendor carefully.

Order Quantities and Reorder Points

Never order more than one year's supply of any form at a time because it may need to be revised unexpectedly. Circumstances beyond your control may make even the perfect form obsolete. For example, the phone company might change the area code for your region, or your company might be acquired by another and be renamed. If a form is very heavily used, you may wish to order less than a year's supply to minimize storage costs or allow you the flexibility to modify it during the year.

After you've decided how many forms to order, you need to set an appropriate reorder point. Then when the supply room notifies you that that point is reached, you have ample time to get a new shipment in without the form's being out of stock. To set a reorder point, consider the following:

- The time needed for users to approve a reprint or request changes
- The time needed to implement any changes and place the order

- The time needed to print the form on a normal, not rush, basis (to avoid overtime charges, if at all possible)
- Amount of safety stock (one month's supply of the old forms still on hand when the new ones are delivered)
- Any seasonal variations in usage

Setting the reorder point at three months' supply usually works well, but for heavily used or very important forms, it's a good idea to calculate the reorder point on a case-by-case basis using the criteria just listed.

Eliminating Obsolete Forms

Ideally, users should notify you when a form becomes obsolete. However, if you wait for that to happen, you'll soon have a supply room full of obsolete forms. Consequently, you need to take the initiative. A good policy is to check with users regarding all forms that have not been ordered for two years to see if they are still in use. When a form is discontinued, destroy any leftover blank copies, and do not reuse the form number.

Bootleg Forms

Probably the most frequent forms control problem arises from "bootleg" forms—forms that users design and print on their own without consulting the forms management group. In addition to being expensive and often poorly designed, bootleg forms may duplicate other forms already in existence.

Sometimes bootleg forms come about because the forms management group is not service-oriented and requesting a new form becomes a bureaucratic nightmare. Or a user may think, "I only need a few copies, so why bother with forms management?" But whatever the reason, the problem is a recurrent one, and a multifaceted approach to solving it is needed.

First, forms management must view itself as a service group. Requesting and getting a new form should be a simple, pleasant, and speedy process. Second, the print shop and purchasing department must accept only those forms orders that have been approved by forms management.

Following these steps will eliminate many bootleg forms. However, users can still develop forms on their personal computers and photocopy them. While you'll never totally eliminate this problem, you can reduce it through the use of a departmental forms coordinator—an individual similar to a records coordinator who serves as a liaison between department members and the forms group. In fact, the same person often serves as both forms and records coordinator.

In addition to notifying forms management of obsolete forms and changes needed in existing forms, the coordinator always is on the lookout for bootleg forms. The coordinator's job is not to police or criticize bootleggers but simply to set up a meeting between them and forms management. If necessary, the bootleg form can be incorporated into the system; otherwise, it should be replaced by an existing form.

On-Line Forms

If you have a networked computer system, make the system work for you. Many companies keep commonly used forms on-line. Users can then fill out the form on their terminal and print copies as needed. Of course, users cannot alter the form itself. Such a system eliminates stocking and ordering forms and ensures that employees always use the latest version of the form.

13

Reports Management— Controlling the Latest Paperwork Explosion

While forms are perhaps the most obvious cause of excess paperwork, another formidable contender—the report—has entered the arena. With data processing, we can now classify, arrange, and present large masses of information in virtually an infinite number of combinations. As a result the average manager is inundated with reports—some of great importance, others not worth the paper they're written on.

The report has also become a corporate status symbol for insecure managers who feel they need to be on every distribution list to demonstrate their importance in the corporate hierarchy. Thus, in many organizations, the report has moved from being a useful information tool to a major problem area. Reports management reverses that trend by controlling the production of reports and ensuring that they provide the maximum benefit to the organization.

What Kinds of Reports?

Since we've identified computer-generated reports as the major cause of the reports explosion, it might seem logical to assume that reports management should deal exclusively with them. However, the scope of the program should be broadened to include all manually generated reports sent between departments on a regular basis. Why? Because although they are fewer in number, manually generated reports waste a great deal of time and money.

Here's a classic example. At one company, the president decides to send the board of directors a monthly report on the company's progress. Sounds like a good idea, doesn't it? Well, in a little over a year, the report grows from 15 pages to over 100. It becomes a competition between the eight vice-presidents to see who can write the longest section and include the most graphs. The legal department takes four pages just to explain that there have been no changes in the cases in litigation.

Each month editing and printing the report ties up the corporate communications staff for over a week, and the last-minute changes reduce the print shop to chaos. As so often happens, the recipients' needs have been forgotten by the producers of the report. One board member, when asked for his opinion, says, "I have my own business to run. I don't have time to read all this." A much better alternative would have been to prepare a concise two- or three-page summary of key events over the past month.

In addition to ego trips like this report, you'll find other manual reports that, with a little assistance, can be generated much more efficiently on a computer. The preparer of the report simply needs to know how to set it up on a personal computer or how to download the data from the mainframe.

When you evaluate manual reports, don't worry about one-time or intradepartmental reports, such as a comparative analysis of some new software or an employee's monthly progress report to his or her boss; these are best left to the discretion of the individual manager. Your concern is with the reports that consume significant amounts of time and money.

Objectives of Reports Management

Just as with forms management, your two primary goals in reports management are to improve efficiency and save money. You can achieve these goals by doing the following:

1. *Eliminating unnecessary reports.* All too many reports are still produced long after the need for them has ended. Your initial reports management effort must clean house to eliminate all such reports. Thereafter, all reports must be regularly reevaluated and their continued existence justified.

2. *Consolidating reports whenever possible.* Are several departments receiving similar reports? If so, investigate the possibility of consolidating them. Demonstrating how consolidation saves money will help motivate departments to work with you.

3. *Redesigning the contents of reports to increase their effectiveness.* Such redesign can include the elimination of unnecessary data, the addition of useful information such as summary data, or the rearrangement of items so they'll be easier for the user to work with. One caution, though: With computer-generated reports, you must compare the cost of making the change with the benefits it provides. Sometimes a change that seems simple may be costly to implement because of the way the initial programming was done or because that programming was never properly documented. So be realistic here.

4. *Limiting distribution of reports when appropriate.* Everyone who receives a report should need it to do his or her job. If the need isn't there, the report shouldn't be either. Actually, many people appreciate this aspect of reports management. They often realize that they don't need a report but won't say so for fear it would appear that they're not doing their jobs as thoroughly as they might.

For managers who have no real need for a report except to check it occasionally, or who feel that they'll lose status if they don't have access to it, there's a simple solution: Keep copies of all reports on file at the company library or information center. Then if these managers do want to see a report occasionally, they can. This solution also allows managers to reduce their in-office active storage of these reports.

5. *Limiting the number of copies produced.* There's a tendency on the part of many managers to order excessive copies of a report. However, if people don't need to see it immediately after it is run or won't be working extensively from it, copies can be routed or shared. For example, a manager might decide she needs five copies of a report—one each for Kathy, Joe, Mandy, and Francine, and one for the files. But if Kathy and Joe share one copy, which is then filed while Mandy and Francine share a second, three copies are eliminated.

6. *Reducing the frequency of reports when appropriate.* Some reports are produced more often than necessary. At one company, sales reports were produced daily, weekly, and monthly, but the users worked only with the weekly and monthly versions. Hence, eliminating the daily report was a logical step. Also some users didn't need the weekly report. Another easy change was sending them the monthly copy only. Instances like these are not uncommon. There's a tendency to base a report's frequency on how often we are capable of preparing it instead of how often we need it.

7. *Using COM and/or COLD when appropriate.* As discussed in Chapters 10 and 11, reports can be stored on microfiche or optical disk, saving both space and money while improving retrieval speed.

8. *Eliminating the hard-copy report altogether by storing data on-line.* Let users reference reports on their terminals. That way, they print only the portions they need.

Selling the Reports Management Concept

Selling reports management to upper management is relatively easy because of the program's cost-effectiveness. Most organizations don't know what they're spending on reports. Once they become aware of that cost, and once they realize reports management can usually save a minimum of 10 percent of that figure (and probably much more), they become quite receptive to the idea. Also, as senior managers usually get the heaviest barrage of reports, they know they have problems coping with the influx of data. Thus, they tend to welcome help.

Just as with records management in general, you can sell the reports management program more easily if you find and document one or two horror stories. Look for some high-cost reports that are overdistributed and poorly designed, and show how they can be improved and what the resulting cost savings are. Explain that you want to apply that same concept on a larger scale, concentrating on those reports that cost the most to produce.

While most middle managers will be receptive to the program, a few may fear that you're taking over their reports and trying to limit the information they receive. Stress that your goal is to make information more accessible and more economical. Also, if their departments are charged back for the reports they receive, they'll be more receptive to the program. It will also help if your department has already gained credibility and trust through the successful implementation of other aspects of records management.

Where to Begin

A reports management program begins in much the same way as forms management or records retention—with an inventory. Collecting these data is easy because most reports are generated by one department—the data processing (or systems) group.

If your program is to be successful, your group must work closely with the systems staff. In fact, in some companies, reports management is a data processing responsibility. However, assigning the responsibility to the systems group often means that manually prepared reports are excluded from the program. Hence, it's usually best if the program is a team effort.

The systems staff should be able to provide you with the following data for each report they run:

- Report number
- Title

- Department(s) requesting the report
- Frequency of distribution
- Distribution list
- Cost of producing and distributing the report

Then, for each report, either you or the systems staff should contact the department(s) requesting the report to determine its purpose. A form similar to the one shown in Exhibit 13-1 can be used to collect these data.

The same types of information will need to be collected for manually prepared reports. The one area in which they will differ from computer-generated reports is cost of preparation. With manual reports, you'll need the hours of employee time spent preparing the report. These hours can then be converted to dollars by using standard hourly rates for each job category, which you can obtain from the human resources department; do make sure an allowance for fringe benefits is included.

Ranking the Reports

Once you've collected the survey data, rank the reports according to the cost of producing them. Ranking is important because you'll want to concentrate your primary efforts on the most costly reports. It's not practical to spend from ten to twenty hours redesigning a report that costs a few hundred dollars a year to produce; you may simply want to determine whether or not it is necessary to continue producing it. On the other hand, if the report costs several thousand dollars a year, the time spent redesigning it is easy to justify.

Contacting the Recipients

The next step is contacting the users of the reports. You'll probably want to schedule one-session interviews with senior managers to discuss all the reports they receive. However, you can simply send the other users a questionnaire similar to the one shown in Exhibit 13-2, explaining in your cover letter that if you

Exhibit 13-1.   Sample Reports Inventory Form.

REPORTS INVENTORY			
Report Title	**Report Number**		
Dept. Requesting or Originating Report			
Purpose of Report: _____			
	Distribution (indicate if more than one copy sent)		
Frequency ☐ daily ☐ semianually ☐ weekly ☐ annually ☐ monthly ☐ other _____	**Name**	**Department**	**No. of Copies**
Cost (use average figures)			
Data processing costs _____ Printing/Photocopying _____ Mailing _____ Graphics _____ Word processing _____ Other _____ _____			
Total _____			
Time (do *not* include EDP time computed above) Hrs. managerial _____ Hrs. secretarial _____ Hrs. clerical _____ Hrs. other _____			
Completed by		Dept.	Date

Exhibit 13-2. Sample Report Recipient Questionnaire.

REPORT RECIPIENT QUESTIONNAIRE		
To be completed by report recipient or interviewer		
Report Title		Report No.
Recipient	Department	Phone

1. Do *you* still need the report? ☐ Yes ☐ No

   a. If "yes," explain briefly how you use the report.

   _____

   _____

   b. If "no," don't complete remainder of form.

2. Do *you* need to receive the report as frequently as you do now?

   ☐ Yes ☐ No

   If "no," how frequently do you need to see the report?

   ☐ daily ☐ monthly ☐ annually

   ☐ weekly ☐ semiannually ☐ other _____

3. How can this report be improved? _____

   _____

   _____

   _____

   _____

   _____

   _____

Prepared by	Date

don't receive a reply by a certain date (usually two or three weeks later), you'll assume that they no longer need the report and will drop them from the distribution list.

The questions on the form are fairly self-explanatory. If recipients indicate that they just review the report and don't base any action on it, sharing a routed copy or having access to a library copy will probably meet their needs. Many people will welcome the opportunity to shed painlessly the reports they don't need.

Taking Action

After you've received all of the responses from users, you can begin taking appropriate action. If no one needs the report, eliminate it entirely. If someone doesn't need the report, drop him or her from the distribution list. In short, look for the "quick fixes"—actions that can be taken easily and which will result in immediate benefits. After you've completed these quick fixes, document the cost savings and report to management on the program's progress to date.

Now you can address the changes in content and design. For multiuser reports, you may need to schedule some meetings to make sure everyone's needs are met. Again, after the changes have been implemented, document the cost savings and productivity improvements and report to management.

Be realistic about the change process. If, as is so often the case, the systems staff is overworked and understaffed, it may take time and continual follow-up to get even relatively simple changes made.

An Ongoing Program

To avoid having to repeat this entire process in two or three years, reports management should be made an ongoing program. A key aspect of this program is the policy that all computer-generated and interdepartmental manual reports that are prepared repeatedly must be approved by the reports management function.

Likewise, all proposed changes in a report's distribution, frequency, or contents must be cleared through reports management.

The steps just outlined are a good start for an ongoing program, but they aren't enough. If users of a form won't notify you when they no longer need it, neither will users of a report. Thus, every two years, reevaluate any report that has not been changed or reviewed in that period. This review is accomplished by sending each recipient the same questionnaire (see Exhibit 13-2) you used when you began the program. Again, your cover letter should explain that recipients will be removed from the distribution list if they don't reply in a timely manner.

Sometimes you can use the "see if anyone notices it's gone" strategy: Simply don't send out the report and see who calls to complain. Those who don't complain are removed from the distribution list. While this technique has worked successfully for many companies, be sure you have appropriate management support before using it. And don't try it with any reports that are clearly vital to the organization's operations and well-being.

All in all, reports management is one of the easiest aspects of records management to promote. It is cost-effective, and top management sees its benefits directly as the number of reports it has to cope with diminishes.

14

Documenting the Records Management Program

Having a well-designed records management program is not enough. You must also communicate the system to its users and to those who will help you implement it. The records manual is your communications vehicle.

Manuals are a problem area in most companies. All too often they become glorified dust catchers, which are never opened by the users—perhaps because users are so often ignored when the manuals are written.

Identifying the Records Manual's Users

To ensure that your manual is a useful tool, begin by identifying its potential users. Typically, they fall into three main categories.

1. *General users of the program—anyone in the company who works with records.* These individuals have broad general concerns such as "How do I send my old records to storage?" or "Can I throw these records away?"

2. *The individuals who will be responsible for implementing the program in their respective departments.* This group nor-

mally includes departmental records coordinators and the department heads. These individuals need two types of information: (1) an overall understanding of the program and their responsibilities within it and (2) the practical information necessary to implement the program on an ongoing basis.

3. *The staff of the records management department.* In addition to the information needed by the other groups, these individuals must understand the detailed procedures for the internal operations of the records management program—for example, how to assign box numbers to records going into storage or how to enter the appropriate information in the index database.

One caution: Don't forget to write down the staff procedures. I've often heard it said, "We're a small department, and we know what we're doing, so why waste time writing it down?" Well, small departments are the most vulnerable. I could cite several instances where the only person who knew how to perform the procedure was taken ill or left abruptly, causing major problems.

So how do you meet all of these special interests without either overwhelming everyone with a monster manual that documents all the program's details or writing three separate manuals? The answer is to develop a "core" manual and build upon it.

General users receive only the core manual, which contains the overall policies, the general procedures, and other information they need in order to comply with the program. In addition to the core manual, the records coordinators and department heads also receive any specific procedures they must comply with, such as how to submit proposed changes to the retention schedule or request that records be microfilmed. Of course, the records management staff receives internal as well as external procedures. You may want to print the procedures for the records coordinators and your staff on different colors of paper to differentiate them clearly.

Issuing the Manual in Sections

Because developing a comprehensive records management program takes time, it is appropriate that the manual be developed in conjunction with each phase of the program as it is implemented instead of after the entire program is operational. Therefore, the section order of the records manual will depend on how your program has evolved. For example, if your program began with records retention, the first three sections of the manual to be issued would be titled (1) Records Management Policy, (2) Records Retention, and (3) Records Center.

Records Management Policy

The policy section of the manual is usually the same for all three categories of users. It should state the organization's overall philosophy of records management. The overall policy statement might be as follows:

> XYZ Company's policy is to maintain a companywide records management program to manage the retention, storage, and protection of the company's records in an efficient, economical manner.
>   The records management program's objectives are to ensure that:

> - The company retains records only as long as needed for administrative, legal, fiscal, or historical purposes.
> - Records are transferred to off-site storage when they become inactive.
> - Document imaging technologies such as microfilm and optical disk are used to enhance records retrieval and use and to conserve space.
> - Vital records are protected from destruction or loss through duplication or other means.

Then you would list the responsibilities of key personnel involved in the program—for example, the records manager, any supervisors reporting to the records manager, the department heads, and the departmental records coordinators. The statements of responsibility can be taken and condensed from the job descriptions for the various positions, with the exception of the department heads, whose responsibilities you would list as follows:

1. To ensure that the records management program is fully implemented in their areas, in compliance with corporate policies and procedures
2. To appoint records coordinators for their areas
3. To ensure that these coordinators have the time and resources needed to perform their job

Spelling all this out may seem to be belaboring an obvious point, but it is important for department heads to realize that the records management policy is just as important as any other corporate policy they must comply with.

The policy section might also include a "whom to contact" page for users with questions about a particular aspect of the program. If you use job titles, not names, the information is less likely to become outdated. Also, if you have an overall corporate policy manual, you may want to include the records management policy in it.

Records Retention

The records retention section of the manual includes information on how to use the retention schedule, the procedure for requesting an addition, deletion, or change to the schedule, and the schedule itself. In the records management staff version, you will probably want to include the procedure for updating the schedule annually. If the records coordinators are involved in the updating procedure, their version should include a procedure specifying their role.

The Records Center

The core version of this section states the center's purpose (storage of inactive records in accordance with the official retention policy). It also gives the procedures for transferring records to the center, requesting records from the center, and destroying records at the end of their retention periods. If the coordinators serve as a central clearing point for departmental users sending records to storage, you'll need to explain what steps they must take before sending the records on.

The contents of this section will depend heavily on whether

you use a commercial records center or operate your own facility. If you operate your own center, you'll need extensive internal staff procedures on such areas as indexing records, assigning box numbers, retrieval of records, and follow-up on checked-out records. If you use a commercial facility, the staff procedures will be much briefer and will coordinate with the vendor's internal procedures.

Other Sections of the Manual

As you expand the program, other sections will be added to the manual, for example: Vital Records; Filing Systems; Document Imaging; Forms Management; and Reports Management.

Vital Records

Here you have a choice. You can incorporate the vital records material in the records manual, or you can include it in the disaster recovery manual (assuming one exists) and simply reference it in the records manual. Whichever alternative you elect, this section should include:

- The company's official definition of a vital record
- The procedure for determining if a record is vital, including a discussion of the vital records committee's role in the process
- The procedure for duplicating records and sending them off-site to the vital records center
- The vital records schedule
- The procedure for retrieving records if necessary

General users and coordinators need to know what records are vital and what their responsibilities are in terms of protecting them. The records management staff also needs details of the day-to-day operations of the program.

Filing Systems

The contents of this section depend on the types of controls you have in place for filing active records. If there is a central files program, procedures for sending records to central files, retrieving them, and returning them should appear in all three versions of the manual. The section for the records management staff should also include the procedures for the internal operation of the central file room.

If there is a uniform filing system, this section should list the various classifications in the system and their definitions and include an index to the system. If the uniform system is used on a decentralized basis instead of in a central file room, the core manual should explain how to implement the system on a departmental basis. On the other hand, if each department maintains its own files without the benefit of a uniform filing system, simply list some general filing guidelines and tips.

If files audits will be conducted, state the procedures that will be followed, the standards that must be met, and the follow-up for departments not in compliance. The core manual should also state the company's policy on purchasing filing equipment, a key part of which should be that the records manager *must* approve all requests for new equipment and that requests will be approved only if the department is in compliance with the retention schedule.

Document Imaging

Whether imaging is micrographics or optical disk or both, the internal operational procedures will be extremely detailed; it may be better to include them in a separate manual. The general user, on the other hand, needs to know how to retrieve and use records on the imaging system, as well as how to request that records be converted to a nonpaper medium.

Forms and Reports Management

While forms management and reports management should each have a section of its own, the contents of both will be very similar. The core manual section begins with an official policy statement that forms (reports) can be created only with the knowledge and authorization of the records management staff. Then it goes on to define forms (reports) and lists the following procedures:

- Requesting new forms or reports
- Requesting changes in existing forms and reports
- Discontinuing existing forms and reports

In addition to this material, the section for the records management staff will include all the internal working procedures in both areas, such as for assigning form numbers and reordering forms. Typically, there will be fewer internal procedures for reports management, as most of these procedures fall under the jurisdiction of the systems department.

Preparing the Manual

Whatever topics you choose to include in the records manual, the preparation process remains basically the same. Preparing a records manual is simpler than preparing other types of administrative manuals for two reasons. First, you are the source of most of the data for the manual. Second, there is less text to write because the retention schedule comprises a major portion of the manual.

Writing the manual will be simpler if you think about it from the program's onset. Take a large file folder, label it "records manual," and drop in any materials that will be useful when it's time to start writing—for example, your memo to senior management explaining what the program will accomplish becomes the nucleus of a policy statement. Then, when you start to draft the manual, much of the data you need will already be gathered in one place.

Physical Appearance

Although you will sometimes see records manuals prepared as bound booklets, this is not advisable because updating the manual will be virtually impossible. A three-ring binder is a more long-lasting and practical approach. In terms of the binder's size, while you want to allow additional space for updates, you also want the manual to be "user friendly." Four-inch binders are difficult to handle and visually intimidating. Therefore, I suggest a 2½-inch maximum width. If the manual won't fit in this size binder (which is highly unlikely), then put it into two volumes.

Make sure the title appears on the binder's spine; that way, it can be clearly identified. And avoid binders with pockets on the inside covers; users have a regrettable tendency to "file" updates to the manual in these pockets. For easy referencing, identify each section of the manual with a Mylar-reinforced index tab that states both the section number and title (e.g., "2. Records Retention"). The holes on the tab sheets should also be Mylar-reinforced.

Each page of the manual should have a standard page heading that clearly identifies it as part of the records manual. Then if a page is removed from the manual, it can easily be replaced in the proper position. If your company has other manuals with standard page headings, model yours on those. Otherwise, you can develop a simple page design similar to the one shown in Exhibit 14-1.

The subject line in Exhibit 14-1 refers to the specific topic, such as "Transferring Records to the Records Center." The number is usually a two-part reference to the section and specific topic. For example, 2-3 refers to the third topic in the second section. Each topic is also page-numbered separately, beginning with page 1. Then if we expand 2-3 from two pages to four, the pages in 2-4, 2-5, and so on will not have to be renumbered.

Each page should also include the date on which that page was issued. When the page is revised, the date is changed accordingly. Then it's a simple matter for users to compare the dates and determine which page is most current.

The Table of Contents

A table of contents, a listing of sections and topics in the order in which they occur, serves as a reference guide to the entire manual. For example, the table of contents for section 2 might read as follows:

2   RECORDS RETENTION
2-1   How to Use the Retention Schedule
2-2   Additions, Deletions, and Changes to the Schedule
2-3   General Records Categories; Duplicate Records
2-4   Records Retention Schedule

Exhibit 14-1. Sample page design for records manual.

⬦ Logo	**RECORDS MANUAL**	Number:
		Page:
	Subject:	Date:

Unlike other manuals, a records manual does not normally need an index. That's because the table of contents is self-explanatory and relatively short, and because the retention and vital records schedules form their own index through listings in order of department number and then alphabetically.

Writing Clearly and Concisely

If the manual is to be a success, the text must be clear and concise. The records manual is not the place for pompous, lengthy sentences extolling the virtues of the records program. Two simple rules will help you avoid that problem:

1. Write in the active voice.
2. Eliminate deadwood.

Writing in the active voice means that the subject of the sentence performs the action. For example:

List each carton separately on the records transfer list. [*"You" is the subject and is understood.*]

or

The central files supervisor completes the report monthly. [*"The supervisor" is the subject.*]

The active voice is concise, and it always assigns responsibility—a must in a manual. The difference becomes obvious if you rewrite the examples above in the passive voice, with the subject being acted upon.

Each carton should be listed separately on the records transfer list.

or

The report is completed monthly. [*"By the central files supervisor" may be added.*]

The other key to good writing is eliminating deadwood, or unnecessary words. Make sure every word is there for a reason.

For example, why say *in the event that* or *due to the fact that* when *if* and *because* will do the job much better? Also avoid repetitious phrases such as *plan in advance* and *basic essentials*.

Playscript Procedures

Much of the writing you'll be doing in the manual is procedural—how to do something. Since most of these procedures involve more than one person, you'll find it helpful to write them in "playscript."* In other words, write the procedure as if it were the script for a play. The only difference is that the "actors" perform specific tasks in the procedure instead of speaking lines of dialogue (see Exhibit 14-2).

As you can see, playscript forces you into a concise, logical writing style. It also makes it easy for each individual to identify his or her responsibilities. An exception or other option is broken out and listed separately, just as is done in item 2a in the exhibit.

Do note the column proportions shown in Exhibit 14-2. Limiting the responsibility column to 2 inches is necessary if you are to have an adequate line length for the actions.

Forms in the Manual

Any forms mentioned in the manual should be reproduced in it. This lets users know what each form looks like and ensures that they use the right one. For example, the playscript procedure just presented would include as an attachment a filled-in sample of Form 269-B placed at the end of the procedure.

Producing the Manual

Of course, you'll want to prepare the manual on a word processor so that it can be updated easily. But proofread the numbers carefully! While the spelling checker feature on most word processing packages is marvelous, it cannot detect a typographical error

*Playscript was developed by Leslie Matthies and is discussed in his book *The New Playscript Procedure* (Stamford, Conn.: Office Publications, Inc., 1977).

Exhibit 14-2. Example of a playscript procedure.

⟨Logo⟩ **RECORDS MANUAL**   Number: 3–3
                                               Page: 1

Subject: Requesting a Record From the Records Center   Date: 8/20/x1

Responsibility   Action

Requester   1. Completes Records Request Form (269-B).

                        2. Sends completed form to records center.

                           a. May also call in request.

Records Center   3. Finds record's location in index.
Coordinator
                           a. If record is not in index, notifies
                              requester.

                        4. Gives blue copy of 269-B to warehouse-
                           person.

Warehouseperson   5. Retrieves record from carton.

                        6. Replaces record with OUT card (blue copy
                           of 269-B in pocket).

Records Center   7. Attaches pink copy of 269-B to record.
Coordinator
                        8. Sends record to requester.

                        9. Files white copy of 269-B in tickler file
                           under date two weeks later.

                2"   4"
[←——————————→] [←————————————————————→]

in the numbers on the retention schedule; and if the correct retention is 5 years and "3 years" is keyed in by mistake, the results
could be disastrous.

Distributing the Manual

Sending the manual out in the mail with a cover letter is a virtual
guarantee that it will be ignored. People are busy, and they'll put
it to one side, saying, "I'll look at it when I have some free time,"
which, of course, they never have.

The best way to distribute the manual is at training sessions
where you can "walk" the users through the manual section by
section, highlighting key points and explaining the rationale behind the various policies. It's a good idea to have separate training sessions for management, coordinators, and other users, as
each group's needs and interests will be different.

Keeping the Manual Up-to-Date

Any manual quickly loses its effectiveness if it's not kept up-to-
date. As already discussed, the retention schedule should be
reviewed annually to incorporate new records and reduce retention values. You should also review the remainder of the manual
annually for two reasons: (1) to pick up the procedural changes
that were not incorporated into the manual when they occurred
and (2) to reassess existing policies and determine if they are still
appropriate.

Don't delegate this task. You'll be surprised at the changes
you'll find—even when you think the manual is up-to-date.
However, it's a good backup to have other staff members review
appropriate sections. They may catch corrections you've overlooked.

Updating the manual also involves making sure users keep
their copies up-to-date. If you're making major revisions, have
users bring their manuals to a training session. The new pages
can be given out and reviewed, and everyone can update his or
her manual at that time. You may also want to include a spot
check of manuals in any departmental files audits.

15

The Future of Records Management

This chapter explores the future of records management in two ways. The first is the program's future within your organization; the second is the future of records management in the United States.

A key concern for any records manager is keeping the program alive within his or her area. You must actively promote the program, keeping both users and management aware of its benefits.

Resuscitating a Comatose Program

Although it is easier to promote and maintain a program that you developed, you may have been placed in the unfortunate position of inheriting a dormant program that was developed internally by someone else. This situation is actually more difficult than starting a program from scratch. With a new program, people are willing to give you the benefit of the doubt.

However, if a program has been allowed to sink into oblivion, you must begin from day 1 to rebuild its credibility. The following is a good approach to take.

1. Identify any service problems users may be experiencing, and make every effort to correct them as quickly as possible.
2. Communicate with the users. If records coordinators have not been named, get them on your team as quickly as possible.
3. If the retention schedule has not been revised in the past two years, your first priority should be revising it.
4. Address the storage area. If it is not set up in an orderly manner, begin the housecleaning and indexing process.
5. If your company's vital records are not identified and protected, begin the process of doing so, starting with the most valuable records.
6. Review the current uses of document imaging within the company, and, if appropriate, identify ways to expand the program.
7. Go the extra mile, whenever practical. If you can provide users with a little extra hands-on support, you'll build your credibility more quickly.

As part of this overall process, be sure to take time to find out why the old program was allowed to lapse. Then develop your strategy to ensure that history does not repeat itself.

Keeping Up With Changes

As you develop and strengthen your organization's program, keep track of where records management is going within the United States. Probably the biggest frustration for users is the complex set of legal requirements for records retention. Unfortunately, there is little hope for improvement at this time. While a number of bills to simplify retention requirements have gone before Congress, none have passed, and the agencies keep churning out more legal requirements.

On the positive side, the technological aspect of records management keeps improving. Optical disk systems are rapidly becoming a reality at many organizations. The key here is to make sure you are part of the decision-making team. As discussed earlier, some organizations are making imaging decisions without input from the records management staff. In every case that I'm aware of where the records management staff was not consulted, problems resulted that could have been easily avoided.

On the other hand, it is not realistic to assume that the entire decision on imaging systems will rest with records management. Team input—from the systems group, the potential users, and records management—is needed, along with a careful consideration of the legal issues involved. Make sure that you're qualified to be part of the team. Doing your homework by learning about new technological advances is a big part of the process. Another factor is keeping the users and their needs in mind.

However, as you expand your technological expertise, don't forget the basics. Having a current records retention schedule, protecting vital records, and providing users with top-notch service regardless of the records' media are the keys to a successful program.

Records management has always been a rewarding profession. But today's records managers have tools and resources available that were not even dreamed of ten years ago. The challenge today is blending the tried and true basic concepts with the technological advances to craft a program that is responsive to users' needs while protecting one of your company's most valuable assets—its records.

It's up to you to meet that challenge. Good luck!

Records Management Resources

ACRC (Association of Commercial Records Centers)
P.O. Box 20518
Raleigh, NC 27619
(919) 821-0757

Administrative Management Society
4622 Street Rd.
Trevose, PA 19047
(215) 953-1040

AIIM (Association for Information and Image Management)
1100 Wayne Ave.
Silver Spring, MD 20910
(301) 587-8202

ARMA International (Association of Records Managers and Administrators)
4200 Somerset, Ste. 215
Prairie Village, KS 66208
(913) 341-3808

Association of Contingency Planners
P.O. Box 73-149
Long Beach, CA 90801–0073
(213) 932-3891

Business Forms Management Association
519 S.W. Third Ave., Ste. 712
Portland, OR 97204-2519
(503) 227-3393

Cimtech
The Hatfield Polytechnic
P.O. Box 109
College Lane
Hatfield, Herts AL10 9AB
England

Institute of Certified Records
Managers
P.O. Box 8188
Prairie Village, KS 66208

International Information
Management Congress
345 Woodcliff Dr.
Fairport, NY 14450
(716) 383-8442

International Records Management Council
22243 Miston Dr.
Woodland Hills, CA 91364

Nuclear Information and Records Management Association
80 Eighth Ave., Ste. 303
New York, NY 10011
(212) 683-9221

OASI (Office Automation Society International)
P.O. Box 374
McLean, VA 22101
(703) 821-6650

References

Alphabetic Filing Rules. Prairie Village, Kans.: ARMA International, latest edition.

Bulgawicz, Susan, and Dr. Charles Nolan. *Disaster Prevention and Recovery: A Planned Approach.* Prairie Village, Kans.: ARMA International, 1988.

Cinnamon, Barry. *Optical Disk Document Storage and Retrieval Systems.* Silver Spring, Md.: AIIM, 1988.

Cinnamon, Barry, and Richard Nees. *The Optical Disk—Gateway to 2000.* Silver Spring, Md.: AIIM, 1991.

Clark, Jesse L. *The Encyclopedia of Records Retention.* New York: The Records Management Group, 1990.

Collins, David J., and Nancy N. Whipple. *Using Bar Code—Why It's Taking Over.* Duxbury, Mass.: Data Capture Press, 1991.

Diamond, Susan Z. *Preparing Administrative Manuals.* New York: AMACOM, 1981.

Directory of Information Management Software for Libraries, Information Centers, Record Centers. Studio City, Calif.: Pacific Information, Inc. (Latest edition.)

Disaster Recovery Journal. St. Louis, Mo.: Systems Support, Inc. (All issues will be of interest.)

Fedders, John M., and Lauryn H. Guttenplan. "Document Retention and Destruction: Practical, Legal, and Ethical Considerations." *The Notre Dame Lawyer* (October 1980).

Federal Regulations Involving Records Retention Requirements for Businesses in Canada. Printed and distributed by Association of Records Managers and Administrators, Inc., Box 6587, Station A, Toronto, Ont. M5W 1A0.

Fire Protection for Archives and Records Centers (ANSI/NFPA 232AM). Quincy, Mass.: National Fire Protection Association, 1990.

Glossary of Records Management Terms. Prairie Village, Kans.: ARMA International, latest edition.

Guideline for a Vital Records Program. Prairie Village, Kans.: ARMA International, latest edition.

Guideline to Job Descriptions. Prairie Village, Kans.: ARMA International, latest edition.

Guideline to Records Center Operations. Prairie Village, Kans.: ARMA International, latest edition.

Guide to Record Retention Requirements in the Code of Federal Regulations. Washington, D.C.: U.S. Government Printing Office, latest edition.

How to File and Find It. Lincolnshire, Ill.: Quill Corporation, 1989.

Imaging Technology Report. Larchmont, N.Y.: Microfilm Publishing, Inc. (All issues will be of interest.)

Inform. Silver Spring, Md.: AIIM. (All issues will be of interest.)

Information Management Sourcebook: The AIIM Buying Guide & Membership Directory. Silver Spring, Md.: AIIM. (Published annually.)

Information Media and Technology. Hatfield, Eng.: Cimtech. (All issues will be of interest.)

International Micrographics Sourcebook. Larchmont, N.Y.: Microfilm Publishing, Inc., latest edition.

International Records Retention Survey. Racine, Wis.: IRMC, 1980.

Microcopying ISO Test Chart No. 2—Description and Use in Photographic Documentary Reproduction (ANSI/ISO 3334-1989). Silver Spring, Md.: AIIM, 1989.

Micrographics Newsletter. Larchmont, N.Y.: Microfilm Publishing, Inc. (All issues will be of interest.)

Optical Memory News. San Francisco: Rothschild Consultants. (All issues will be of interest.)

Palmer, Roger C. *The Bar Code Book.* Peterborough, N.H.: Helmers Publishing, Inc., 1989.

Photography (Chemicals)—Residual Thiosulfate and Other Chemicals in Films, Plates, and Papers—Determination and Measurement, ANSI PH4.8-1985. Silver Spring, Md.: AIIM, 1985.

Photography (Film)—Processed Safety Film—Storage, ANSI PH1.43-1985. Silver Spring, Md.: AIIM, 1985.

Practice for Operational Procedures/Inspection and Quality Control of First-Generation Silver-Gelatin Microfilm of Documents, ANSI/AIIM MS23-1990. Silver Spring, Md.: AIIM, 1983.

Protection of Records (ANSI/NFPA 232). Quincy, Mass.: National Fire Protection Association, 1990.

Recommended Practice for Inspection of Stored Silver-Gelatin Microforms for Evidence of Deterioration, ANSI/AIIM MS45-1990. Silver Spring, Md.: AIIM, 1990.

Records Management Quarterly. Prairie Village, Kans.: ARMA International. (All issues will be of interest.)

Saffady, William. Micrographic Systems. Silver Spring, Md.: AIIM, 1990.

———. Optical Disk Systems for Records Management. Prairie Village, Kans.: ARMA International, 1988.

Shiel, Arthur. Optical Disk Storage and Image Processing Systems: A Guide and Directory. Hatfield, Eng.: Cimtech, 1990.

Skupsky, Donald S., ed. Legal Requirements for Business Records. Denver: Information Records Clearinghouse. (Updated annually.)

———. Legal Requirements for Microfilm, Computer and Optical Disk Records. Denver: Information Records Clearinghouse, 1991.

———. Recordkeeping Requirements. Denver: Information Records Clearinghouse, 1990.

Software Directory for Automated Records Management Systems. Prairie Village, Kans.: ARMA International, 1990.

Glossary

active record   A record that is used frequently and needs to be available for immediate access by users.

administrative value   The period of time a record may be needed within the company for administrative or operational purposes.

aperture card   An eighty-column keypunch card designed to hold one frame of 35mm microfilm; primarily used for engineering drawings.

archival value   The permanent retention of a record for historical reasons.

ASCII   An acronym for American Standard for Computer Information Interchange. This is an eight-level code for data that allows 256 code combinations; it was developed to ensure compatibility between all data services.

backup copy   A duplicate of a record retained for reference in case the original is lost or destroyed.

bar code   An automatic identification technology that encodes information into an array of adjacent varying-width parallel rectangular bars and spaces.

blip   A mark on a roll of microfilm (below the image); used to count images or frames automatically.

CAR   Computer-assisted retrieval; primarily used with systems for computer-indexing microfilm for fast retrieval.

card jackets   An index card designed to hold twenty or fewer images on 16mm film, as well as some eyeball-readable data.

cartridge   A container for roll microfilm that protects the film and makes it easier to load it into a reader.

CD-ROM   An optical disk that can be read only; it cannot be written on. Used in applications where a number of copies are made from a master disk.

central files   Files belonging to more than one individual or organizational unit that are physically grouped together.

Certified Office Automation Professional (COAP)   The professional certification program in office automation; managed by the Office Automation Society International.

Certified records manager (CRM)   The professional certification program in records management; managed by the Institute of Certified Records Managers.

chronological filing   Filing in sequence according to date; usually the latest date is in front.

COAP   *See* Certified Office Automation Professional

COM   Computer output microfilm or computer output microfiche; microfilm produced from on-line computer data or off-line tapes through the use of a COM recorder.

commercial records center   A records center operated by a private service company and housing the records of many different companies.

compactible files   An open-shelf filing system where the shelving units are mounted on tracks and can be slid back and forth to open an aisle at the appropriate point.

CRM   *See* certified records manager.

decentralized files   Records located and maintained in or near the department that is immediately responsible for the function they relate to.

density   The opacity or degree of darkness of the background on negative film; measured by a densitometer.

diazo One type of film used for microfilm copies; requires ammonia for processing.

disaster recovery plan A program of activities that should be followed in the event of a disaster. The plan should cover all activities, but the term is used by some organizations to indicate the resumption of computer system operations.

document digitization The use of scanners to convert documents to digitally coded electronic images suitable for optical disk storage.

DRAW (direct read after write) The ability to read an optical disk image immediately after it is recorded.

duplex A method of microfilming that captures in one exposure both the front and back of a document.

Electronic Data Interchange (EDI) The computer-to-computer transfer of standardized information between companies.

electronic mail The electronic transfer of correspondence and memos from one terminal to another.

erasable optical disks A type of optical disk that permits information to be deleted and the reuse of previously recorded disk areas.

file integrity The ability to retrieve and use a document without the chance of its being lost or misfiled.

filing inches File volume measured in linear inches. A standard letter-size file drawer holds 25 filing inches.

fiscal/tax value The period of time a record must be retained for financial reasons or for tax requirements.

forms management The function responsible for the creation, design, revision, and control of all forms within an organization.

hard copy The paper copy of a record.

hardware The mechanical and electronic parts of a computer; also the equipment used in a computer system.

high-density filing system   Any type of filing equipment that permits the storage of large volumes of records in a minimum amount of floor space.

hypo   *See* sodium thiosulfate.

inactive record   A record that does not need to be immediately available but must be retained for legal reasons or because users have an infrequent need to access it.

jacket   A transparent plastic carrier with sleeves for holding strips of microfilm.

jukebox   An automatic selection and retrieval device that provides rapid on-line access to multiple optical disks.

lateral file cabinet   A file cabinet that is wider than it is deep. Records can be arranged either front to back or sideways.

legal value   The period of time a record must be retained to meet statutory requirements or for other legal reasons.

medium   The material or substance on which information is recorded, such as paper, microfilm, magnetic disk or tape, or optical disk.

methylene blue test   A chemical test for determining the level of sodium thiosulfate remaining on film after it is processed.

microfiche   A sheet of microfilm, approximately 4 by 6 inches, with the images arranged in a grid pattern.

microfilm   A fine-grain, high-resolution film used to record images reduced in size from the original.

microforms   The various forms of microfilm.

micrographics   The art or technology of microfilming.

mobile aisle system   *See* compactible files.

optical character recognition (OCR)   An automatic data entry system that uses human-readable, squared-off alphanumeric symbols that can be scanned and read by special scanning equipment.

optical disk A special disk that can store large amounts of information through encoding by a laser beam.

OUT **card** A filing card used to replace a checked-out record. It usually indicates who checked out what record and when.

planetary camera A type of microfilm camera in which the film and the document being photographed remain in a stationary position during the exposure.

printout Paper output from a computer.

pulpit ladder A safety ladder having an extended top shelf, used for retrieving records stored on high shelves.

purge Removal from a file of information that is of no further value.

reader A device that enlarges microfilm images for viewing.

reader-printer A device that enlarges microfilm images for viewing and which also can produce a hard copy of the enlarged image.

record Any form of recorded information, regardless of medium.

records center A centralized area for storing inactive records.

records center box A 15- by 12- by 10-inch corrugated cardboard box designed to hold approximately one cubic foot of records, either legal- or letter-size

record series A group of similar or related records, used or filed as a unit.

records inventory A detailed listing of all records categories maintained by an organization. The inventory is usually made as the first step in preparing a records retention schedule.

records management The systematic control of an organization's records from their creation or receipt to their ultimate preservation or destruction.

records manager The individual with the responsibility for controlling the organization's records management program.

records retention schedule   A listing of all of the organization's records categories that specifies the time period each should be retained.

reports management   A system for creating, managing, and disposing of the reports used by an organization.

resolution   (1) A method of measuring the sharpness or clarity of a microfilm image; (2) as applied to optical disk technology, the number of dots per inch or pixels that are scanned.

rotary camera   A type of microfilm camera in which both the document and the film move simultaneously during the filming process.

scanner   A piece of equipment that translates a document into digitized form.

shelf file   Side-open records storage equipment in which the records are accessed horizontally.

shredder   A machine used for the destruction of records by reducing the documents to fine strips, shreds, or particles.

sodium thiosulfate (also called hypo)   A chemical used in processing film. It removes the silver halide remaining in the film after development.

software   The programs that instruct a computer to perform specific functions.

source document   A record in tangible hard-copy form.

statute of limitations   A time period after an event during which a legal action or lawsuit may be initiated.

step-and-repeat camera   Microfilm camera used to produce source document microfiche.

terminal digit filing   A numerical filing system. The file number is divided into groups of two or three digits. A document is filed first by the last group of digits, then by the middle group, and finally by the first group.

tickler file   A file organized by date. Documents or reminder notices are filed under the date on which they should be reviewed or acted upon.

uniform filing system   A standardized subject filing system that is used throughout an organization.

vacuum drying   A method of drying water-soaked records in an "airless" or vacuum chamber. This process is used to save records that have been damaged in a disaster.

vertical file cabinet   Filing equipment that is deeper than it is wide. Records are stored from front to back.

vesicular film   A microfilm used for making duplicate copies. Processing is done by the application of heat.

vital records   Those records that are essential (1) to resume or continue operations in the event of a disaster, (2) to preserve the rights of the organization's owners, employees, and customers, and/or (3) to protect the organization legally and financially.

vital records schedule   A listing of an organization's vital records along with an explanation of how each is to be protected from destruction in the event of a disaster.

WORM (write once, read many times)   A type of optical disk that is not erasable.

Index

[Italic page references refer to figures.]